Culture in Britain since 1945

Making Contemporary Britain

General Editor: Anthony Seldon
Consultant Editor: Peter Hennessy

Institute of Contemporary British History
34 Tavistock Square, London WC1H 9EZ

Culture in Britain since 1945

Arthur Marwick

Basil Blackwell

Copyright © Arthur Marwick 1991

First published 1991

Basil Blackwell Ltd
108 Cowley Road, Oxford, OX4 1JF, UK

Basil Blackwell, Inc.
3 Cambridge Center
Cambridge, Massachusetts 02142, USA

British Library Cataloguing in Publication Data

A CIP catalogue record for this book is available from the British Library.

Library of Congress Cataloging in Publication Data

Marwick, Arthur, 1936–
    Culture in Britain since 1945/Arthur Marwick.
        p.   cm.
    Includes bibliographical references and index.
    ISBN 0–631–17189–4 (hard) — ISBN 0–631–17191–6 (paper)
    1. Great Britain–Popular culture–History–20th century.
    2. Great Britain–Intellectual life–1945– 3. Great Britain–Civilization–
    1945– I. Title.
    DA589.4.M37   1991
    941.085–dc20   90–46425
                                                              CIP

Typeset in Ehrhardt on 11/13 pt
by Setrite Typesetters Ltd.
Printed in Great Britain by Billing & Sons Ltd., Worcester

This book is dedicated,
with love,
to Tracey Leahy

Contents

List of Illustrations

2 Tradition, War and Consensus

The great complex movement dominating the arts in the twentieth century is that of Modernism, among whose characteristics (not all characteristics being displayed by all practitioners) are: (a) a conviction that a new era of cataclysmic change demands a new art; (b) a rejection of *mimesis* (imitation of the 'real' world), representationalism (direct representation of nature) and figurism (direct representation of human figures or objects); (c) the explicit and self-conscious recognition that the arts are an artificial convention or game (consisting of words on a page, paint on a canvas etc.); and (d) the conviction that instead of merely echoing 'reality', art should create a separate 'reality' of its own. Modernism could at times entail a quite shocking disruption of the order, sequences and harmonies of traditional forms.[1]

The full extent and nature of the effects the war experience had on the different facets of British society and culture are a matter of considerable debate among historians; but whatever wider views are held about historical causation, it is impossible to ignore the complicated legacy of the war as an important influence on subsequent developments. Britain was both a heroic victor, the country which had 'fought alone', and a country clearly reduced in status (though its rulers preferred to continue to avert their eyes from that unpleasant fact) to well below that of the two emergent super-powers, America and Russia; America, and the Americans, were now a more immediate and compelling presence than ever before. For many artists war is in itself an outrage, for some having a special horror of its own, for others simply confirming their sense that the current century is a century of catastrophe and cruelty. Already at the time of the First World War intellectuals had come to see that only the modes of modernism were adequate to grappling with the cruelty and the outrage, and that the only proper reactions were of isolation and despair. But the Second World War had another face as well: that of a 'people's war', of partisans and resistance workers, of all classes and many nations united against the unspeakable nastiness of Nazism. Should art then not come back to the people rather than cut itself off in the most abstruse forms of modernism?

Wars quicken the pulse. That small, but potentially influential, group of people who think about these things at all, thought it important to show that in fighting Nazism, Britain was fighting for the finest in European and British cultural traditions. Against the hostility of reactionaries and 'realists', the Council for the Encouragement of Music and the Arts (CEMA) was established as an agency for subsidizing the arts. Myra Hess, the distinguished concert pianist, put on her famous lunch-time recitals in the National Gallery in London; the Sadler's Wells opera company, driven out of that same London by the bombing of its theatre, carried opera around the provinces. Civil servants evacuated from London created new local demands for high-, or at least middle-brow culture. Benjamin Britten, the composer, and Peter Pears, the tenor, willingly returned to Britain in the spring of 1942 after having followed Auden to America in 1939, were not alone in feeling that Britain in wartime was undergoing a cultural renaissance.[2] In 1946 CEMA was established on a long-term basis as the Arts Council, while the new Labour government made it possible (clause 132 of the 1948 Local Government Act) for local authorities to raise sixpence in the pound on the rates in order to support local cultural enterprises. A number of local theatres were established very much as direct reaction to the war experience.

It is not inaccurate to speak of a raising of consciousness in wartime, among the workers, among women, and indeed among some members of the various sections of the middle classes who, as never before, felt some responsibility towards the denizens of the country's slums. None the less, in the British general election of 1945 20 per cent of the electorate (since 1928, all men and all women aged twenty-one and over) did not feel sufficiently interested or involved to vote at all (great efforts had been made to ensure that servicemen, many still far from home, should have their votes counted); 39 per cent of those who did participate voted Conservative — in all kinds of ways Britain was and remained a deeply conservative nation; but, with the working class voting in a more unified way than ever before, and with about one-third of the entire middle-class vote going to Labour, that party gained 47.8 per cent of the vote. Because of the nature of the British electoral system this resulted in Labour, for the first time, having not just a majority, but an overwhelming majority, in Parliament. Labour actually increased its popular vote in the general elections of both 1950 and 1951, and in the latter election still held a plurality in the country as a whole. But this time the electoral system allowed the Conservatives in with a small majority. Up till this point, the dominant forces affecting social and cultural development were the general conditions of austerity resulting from the heavy losses sustained during the war, and the very positive efforts of the Labour government to make Britain a more equal society through high taxation, controls of various sorts, and the deliberate development of social services on a quite unprecedented scale. The official ideology was of 'fair shares', equal citizenship and pulling together in order to win the 'export drive' necessary if Britain was to free itself from a dependence on American subsidy. If there were alternative ideologies, the most evident was that which reacted against rationing and controls, and what were seen as regimentation and misguided attempts to impose equality; there are but few manifestations of any ideology embodying a radical or revolutionary critique of the Labour government. Twentieth-century *angst* was given a new and special focus with the development of atomic weapons.

On the whole, the mainstream of the Conservative party came to feel that it had to accommodate to the changes which took place under Labour. It was largely because of a change in world terms of trade that living standards did begin to go up in the fifties; controls were fully relaxed, rationing abolished, and open encouragement given to private enterprise. But broadly a spirit of 'consensus' prevailed (all such generalizations are open to criticism in detail; the point about such words is that they are *comparative*: this period of 'consensus' can profitably be compared with earlier periods of bitter political controversy, and, say, the period since the advent to power of Mrs Thatcher). Within a class structure which was still very recognisably that of: (a) a firmly entrenched upper class, as that class had established itself in the early twentieth century, whose members, if they cared to exercise it, had privileged access to positions of power, influence and wealth; of (b) a variegated middle class, increasing slightly in size with the growth of administrative, professional and clerical occupations, but overall suffering from high taxation; and (c) a working class enjoying better conditions and higher prestige than ever before the ideology of consensus, if I can put it that way, was of a well-disposed, well-educated upper class, cooperating with the various fractions of the middle class, and with certain representatives of the working class, in running the country in the best interests of everyone, it being understood that those interests comprised spending money both on welfare services and, to a degree never envisaged before the war, on culture, that culture being of the types sanctioned by such upper-class experts (they were, in cultural terms, far from reactionaries) as Sir Kenneth Clark and J. M. (by this time, Lord) Keynes. It was an unchallenged assumption that Britain led the world with its Welfare State, that Britain, the home of tolerance and 'seeing the other fellow's point of view' had carried through a 'quiet revolution', and that, since Britain had more to offer the world than the world had to offer to Britain, Britain should now abandon the old reticence, and perhaps inferiority complex, about its own cultural practices. To this parochialism and complacency there were challenges from the very outset. The war, and its immediate aftermath, necessarily involved contacts both with America and with the other European countries. It was partly in the spirit of post-war internationalism that major exhibitions of foreign art came to Britain. Other foreign influences, including that of American rock-and-roll, became pronounced in the fifties. The varying balance, within the different art forms, between parochialism and internationalism will be a major component in the four chapters which follow.

If modernism (sometimes in the form of reactions against it) is the governing force in élite culture, a crucial general influence was that of the new communications technologies, the basis of film, radio and, eventually, television. Certain aspects of modernism itself were directly influenced by the new machine age; on the whole, however, the new mass media tended, though not exclusively, to aim for naturalism, rather than modernistic innovation.

Notes

1 For an excellent summary see, Gabriel Josipovici, 'The Birth of the Modern 1885–1914', conveniently reprinted as chapter 2 of Clive Emsley, Arthur Marwick and Wendy Simpson, *War, Peace and Social Change: A Reader* (1990).
2 Michael Kennedy, *Britten* (1981), pp. 37, 43.

3 Literature and Drama: from Rhetoric to Empiricism

The cosy post-war scene

Poetry is widely conceived of as being more 'difficult' than prose. More difficult to read because its meaning and mood are highly concentrated, word order departs sharply from that of ordinary speech, allusions are rich and often obscure. More difficult to write because poetry deploys a heavy battery of technical effects, principally rhythm, rhyme, metaphor and symbol. Yet where novels are long, poems are short. A poem can be read, reflected upon, partially memorized during the terror and inconvenience of a single air raid; a novel will demand the space of several disrupted nights. Something like a poem can be dashed off, and polished, while off duty on a battleship, while waiting at an air force base for the order to scramble, while crouching in a fox-hole as Rommel's tanks move into position. Much poetry, at any rate, was written during the Second World War, and, as these things go, anthologies of war poetry sold quite well. Alun Lewis (b. 1919), Sidney Keyes (b. 1922) and Keith Douglas (b. 1920) all perished in 1944: Lewis expressed the sense of solitary exile of the soldier, Keyes the cruelty of war, Douglas its futility. Experience in the Royal Navy marked the early poetry of Roy Fuller (b. 1912), Charles Causley (b. 1917) and Alan Ross (b. 1922). Briefly there appeared the 'Apocalyptic Movement' led by J. F. Hendry (b. 1912), Henry Treece (1912–66) and G. S. Fraser

(b. 1915), which proclaimed the primacy of the individual over the mechanization and regimentation of war.

Poetry when the war ended was, as it were, on the map, even if the chief poets of the thirties seemed to have faltered (Auden was in America, MacNeice seemed to have lost his creative energy). *The* poet, perhaps as much because of life style (dissolute) and self-advertisement (brash), was the Welsh neo-Romantic Dylan Thomas, who had been publishing since the early thirties but now set the tone for British poetry in the immediate post-war years − colourful, passionate, full of complex word play. In 1946 came the publication both of Douglas's highly praised posthumous *Alamein to Zem Zem*, and Thomas's widely circulated *Deaths and Entrances*. Thomas's influence is most obviously seen in the poetry of fellow Welshman and life-long friend Vernon Watkins, described by Edward Lucie-Smith as 'romantic and solemn'.[1] Others who can, in the shorthand of this book, be characterized as neo-Romantics, lovers of elaborate language, purveyors of allusions to exotic foreign lands or to the lore of Ancient Athens and Ancient Rome, are Lawrence Durell (b. 1912, man of the Med., and particularly Egypt), George Barker (b. 1913, surrealist in his highly complex imagery), David Gascoyne (b. 1916, 'the only genuine surrealist poet writing in English'[2]) and John Heath-Stubbs (b. 1918, 'imbued with a nostalgia for "classicism" − in itself a romantic characteristic'[3]). Roy Fuller, whose collection *Epitaphs and Occasions* was published in 1949, with his austere language and deliberately intellectual approach, clearly stood apart from the neo-Romantics, while sharing their wide range of reference and romantic treatment of the erotic. Stevie Smith (1902−71), in her *apparent* scatty naivety, defied classification:

> *Our cat Tedious*
> *Still lives,*
> *Count not Tedious*
> *Yet*
>
> *My name is Finis,*
> *Finis, Finis,*
> *I am Finis,*

Six, five, four, three, two
One Roman,
Finis.[4]

On the whole, poets did not achieve the popularity and reputation won by successful novelists and playwrights. Dylan Thomas came near when his (mainly) verse play specially written for radio, *Under Milkwood*, was broadcast (1954) and subsequently given both in the form of solo readings by the author and full dress stage presentation. But as best-known poet Thomas was shortly eclipsed by John Betjeman (1906–87), whose cunning blend of nostalgia and the kind of idiosyncratic humour that the British love to salute (as for instance in the Ealing Studios' films of the time) nicely met the new post-war appetite for poetry: his *Selected Poems* (1948) turned him from minor to best-selling poet. Not, of course, that either of these came close in stature to T. S. Eliot, whose poetry attained its highest reputation at this time.

Novelists to the fore at the end of the war (that is to say noticed in the book pages of the quality newspapers and reviews) were: Evelyn Waugh (1903–66, author, in the thirties, of wickedly funny satires of the old and new rich), Graham Greene (b. 1904, author, in the thirties, of committed left-wing novels), Joyce Cary (1888–1957), C. P. Snow (1905–80), L. P. Hartley (1895–1972), Anthony Powell (b. 1905), Ivy Compton-Burnett (1884–1969, whose first novel had been published in 1928) and Henry Green, pseudonym of Henry Yorke (1905–69). By anyone's definition Powell was upper-class; by my definitions so were Greene, Cary, Hartley, Compton-Burnett and Yorke, while Waugh had succeeded in socializing himself into that class; only Snow stood out, a lower-middle-class lad making his way up as scientist and bureaucrat, eventually to join the upper class. Both Greene and Waugh had become converts to Catholicism. Waugh's work – his war service may have had something to do with this – while still brilliantly witty, became more serious; he was to emerge as one of the most extreme critics of the trends towards social and economic democracy of the war and post-war period – he lamented, when the Conservatives returned to power, that they did not put the clock back by one minute; Waugh had no liking either for the influence and presence of the Americans. *Brideshead Revisited*, a nostalgic, though sometimes sardonic, evocation of the upper-class world of the inter-war years which now seemed to have vanished, was published in 1945. *The Loved One* (1948) was a savage satire on American funeral customs and the ambivalences of America's affluent society. In 1952 came the first of the *Sword of Honour* trilogy, *Men at Arms*; there followed *Officers and Gentlemen* (1955) and *Unconditional Surrender* (1961). At times it seemed that the regimentation, cynicism and muddle of war was being regarded as a betrayal of high conservative principles; but Waugh also got much of the essence of 'the people's war': caught in an air raid, two officers agree: 'We had better leave this to the civilians.'[5].

Of all writers of the era, Graham Greene most completely embodies the puzzles of the relationships between (a) artistic autonomy, integrity and intention and (b) commercial success: from what would seem to be the very depths of his being he drew a passionate commitment to left-wing causes which has never abated; from his Catholicism, an obsession with fundamental evil and fundamental good; from his incredible nose for public affairs, a gift for setting his novels in troubled parts of the world almost before they hit the headlines. Greene's tautly constructed plots are never less than thrilling, their sense of place and time is always impeccable. *The Heart of the Matter* (1948) is set in a west African colony as British colonialism is coming to an end; *The End of the Affair* (1951) evokes the blitz and war-time London in a far more direct way than Waugh's trilogy; *The Quiet American* (1955) offers its own insights into the unfolding of the Indo-China tragedy in the Cold War era. Right throughout our period, with undiminished power, the novels continued to appear, with locations bang ahead of the minute: *Our Man in Havana* (1958), *A Burnt-out Case* (1961), set in a leper colony in the Congo, *The Honorary Consul* (1973), set in Argentina, *The Human Factor* (1978), set in the intelligence services with nice allusions to a Britain in which the whole post-war experiment in socialism and consensus seems to be collapsing. Corporate violence, very much the background to everyone's experience in this era, is ever-present.

In 1944 Joyce Cary published *The Horse's Mouth*, the last in the trilogy built about the splendid characters of the outrageous painter Gully Jimson, and the shrewd, immoral, Sara, which deliberately presented a panorama of certain aspects of English history over the previous sixty years. The post-war trilogy *A Prisoner of Grace* (1952), *Except the Lord* (1953) and *Not Honour More* (1955) dealt more explicitly with political life in the era of before, during and after the First World War. These were moral fables in the great tradition; in turn, we see each of the main characters from inside. C. P. Snow had begun his *Strangers and Brothers* sequence in 1940, its purpose, he said, being to give insights into British society over the period 1920–50 and to follow the *moral* (my italics) growth of Lewis Eliot, the narrator of the series. The series was continued with *The Light and the Dark* (1947), *A Time of Hope* (1949), *The Masters* (1951), *The New Men* (1954), *Homecomings* (1956), *The Conscience of the Rich* (1958), *The Affair* (1959), *Corridors of Power* (1963), *The Sleep of Reason* (1968), *Last Things* (1970). Snow, it would be widely agreed, could neither present all of his main characters in the round and from the inside, as could Joyce Carey, nor evoke the richness and subtlety of atmosphere of a Graham Greene novel. Snow's works, too often, are 'works', much too consciously social and political documents. In *The Masters*, about the struggle for the mastership of a Cambridge college, Snow *asserts* that one of the candidates is a finer and richer character than the one who actually wins, but he scarcely persuades us of this. For the historian there are many interesting details: in *Homecomings*, Lewis Eliot muses that post-war society 'had become more rigid, not less, since our youth'; *Corridors of Power* was a phrase that entered the ordinary language.

Between 1944 and 1947 L. P. Hartley published his *Eustace and Hilda* trilogy about the destructive relationship between a brother and sister. In *The Go-Between* (1953), an elderly man in 1952 recalls the events of the hot summer of 1900 when, as an innocent child, he unknowingly acted as a go-between carrying letters between two lovers; in effect the child becomes victim. Similar preoccupations appear in *The Hireling* (1957), the chauffeur having a relationship with her ladyship. That Hartley was not at ease in the world of social democracy and the welfare state seems to be demonstrated in *Facial Justice* (1960) which presented an unpleasant vision of a drab, mediocre future in which there was no competition. Henry Green was a highly individualistic writer with a small but loyal following: his *Loving* (1945), *Concluding* (1948), *Nothing* (1950), and *Doting* (1952) are characterized by the very personal use of colloquial language, and by such idiosyncrasies as sentences without verbs, and nouns without articles. Another writer with something of a cult following was Ivy Compton-Burnett. Deliberately mannered and non-naturalistic, set amidst the Edwardian upper class, her novels − for example, *Man Servant* and *Maid Servant* (1947) and *Darkness and Day* (1951) − are about power and cruelty. Henry Green found his milieux in all social classes; C. P. Snow demonstrated some of the ways in which the upper class recruited from below; but the long-established core elements of the upper class still commanded much attention. In 1951 Anthony Powell launched his somewhat monotone *The Music of Time*, about, he said, 'the numerous varieties of "the best people"', with *A Question of Upbringing*. There followed *A Buyer's Market* (1952), *The Acceptance World* (1955), *Casanova's Chinese Restaurant* (1960) and *The Kindly Ones* (1962).

The two most internationally famous novels of the period came from the scion of an impoverished upper-class family who had deliberately not used his education at Eton to regain social status: known in the thirties for his empathetic studies of workers, down-and-outs, and Catalonia in the Spanish Civil War, George Orwell (pseudonym of Eric Blair, 1903−50) produced the comparatively light satire on totalitarianism *Animal Farm* (1945), followed by the nightmare vision of Fascist dictatorship merged with Stalinist oppression, *Nineteen Eighty-Four* (1949). Some critics, however, identified as one of the great works of the century *Under the Volcano* (1947), part of a projected larger work by the chronic alcoholic Malcolm Lowry, a novel of private hell within the downfall of Western society. Quite specifically British satire of the outmoded upper middle class began to appear in the works of Angus Wilson (b. 1913): *The Wrong Set* (1949), *Such Darling Dodos* (1950), and *Hemlock and After* (1952).

War conditions, and especially long nights in the air-raid shelters, encouraged the reading of novels, and even of poetry; bombs destroyed theatres, or at least placed them under threat. The same novels could be read all over the country, but drama had, before the Second World War, been very much centred on London. Plays aiming at commercial success with the predominantly middle-class and upper-class audiences were the staple of the West End theatres; only a few specialist theatres consciously aimed to put on avant-garde plays for a minority within that same audience. The main theatres in the provincial centres were essentially touring theatres receiving repertory companies, usually London-based, doing standard works, and also West End productions before or after their London runs (there were exceptions, such as the Glasgow Citizens' theatre). The war destroyed or badly damaged one-fifth of London theatres, and fostered the growth of monopoly in theatrical ownership; yet it also helped to stimulate the beginnings of a theatrical revival in the provinces. In 1943 a group of citizens joined together to save the historic Theatre Royal in Bristol, and in 1946 it became an arm of the London Old Vic theatre; the establishment of the Coventry Municipal theatre at the end of the war was essentially a response to the destruction of war and to the desire to build a richer life in the post-war world. At the same time, theatre folk, like everyone else, suffered the restraints and burdens of austerity: on purely commercial productions, 10 per cent of gross receipts was whipped away in entertainments tax. However 'cultural socialism' expressed itself in the exemption given to educational enterprises: Tennent Productions Ltd, for instance, cashed in on this, and put on some 'serious' plays.[6]

In many respects the immediate post-war years were special in that a small group of brilliant classical actors came to their peak – John Gielgud, Ralph Richardson, Donald Wolfit and, above all, Laurence Olivier. Looking back from the sixties, Kenneth Tynan, the dynamic critic who burst on the public scene in 1951, declared: 'We may see their like again, but we shall not see the like of their theatrical careers.'[7] It was still possible for such distinguished figures to run their own companies as actor-managers: Wolfit gave a reason at the

Bedford, Camden Town, in 1949; Olivier gave two seasons at the St James's in 1950 and 1951; and Gielgud gave a season at the Haymarket in 1954–5. For serious theatre-goer and serious producer alike, most opportunities were confined to the classics, and 'the classics' almost always meant Shakespeare. It was in *Measure for Measure* that one of what was to prove a new breed of theatrical producers (soon to be known as *directors*), Peter Brook, established himself. But on the whole, the conditions of production of the thirties, and the playwrights of that era, continued to dominate (with much commercial power in the hands of Prince Littler's consortium, known as 'The Group'). Most popular were J. B. Priestley, Somerset Maugham, Noel Coward and Terence Rattigan. Rattigan was the perfect exponent of the 'well-made play', technically brilliant, often moving in a rather sentimental way, and never expressing any utterance radical enough to disturb the audience: *The Winslow Boy* (1946) concerns the ultimate exoneration, through the dedicated efforts of a very conservative barrister, of a young naval cadet wrongly accused of stealing a postal order; *The Browning Version* (1948) is about a somewhat inadequate school master at a public school; *Separate Tables* (1954) was marginally more daring in its treatment of a social misfit keeping up appearances in a seaside hotel. The 'advanced' alternative was the kind of verse drama which T. S. Eliot had tried to re-establish in the thirties with his *Murder in the Cathedral*. Eliot's own later efforts, *The Cocktail Party* (1949) and *The Confidential Clerk* (1954) were less successful, C. S. Lewis commenting that 'Eliot's stage verse imitates prose, with remarkable success'. Christopher Fry (b. 1907) wrote heady stuff for these years of austerity, full of neo-Romantic rhetoric, which certainly sounded like theatre, even if it did not always look like it: *A Phoenix Too Frequent* (1946), *The Lady's Not for Burning* (1949) and *A Sleep of Prisoners* (1951).

Reactions in the early fifties

As the post-war Labour government began to falter, there was much to react against in the often flamboyant, but altogether very cosy world of literature and drama. In the still tinier world of literary criticism and poetry changes were apparent at the end of the forties. The literary magazine which had linked post-war preoccupations to pre-war ones was *Horizon*, founded in 1939 by thirties poet Stephen Spender and the Eton and Balliol-educated critic Cyril Connolly, who edited it. Connolly brought the magazine to a close in December 1949 with the, perhaps all too characteristically, pretentious words: 'from now on an artist will be judged only by the resonance of his solitude and the quality of his despair'. Already a number of younger poets had determined to make a clear and explicit stand against modernism, internationalism, neo-Romanticism and the exclusiveness of upper-class bohemia. One of them, Kingsley Amis (b. 1922), whose first volume of poems, *Bright November*, had been published in 1947, declared in 1951: 'Nobody wants any more poems about philosophers or paintings or novelists or art galleries or mythology or foreign cities or other poems. At least I hope nobody wants them.'

Another, John Wain (b. 1925), whose collection *Mixed Feelings* appeared in 1951, expressed a revulsion against 'the punch-drunk random "romantic" scribblers' whose verses had filled the poetry magazines in the forties. Wain, then a lecturer at Reading University, used his position on the BBC Third Programme series *First Reading* to publicize such like-minded poets as Donald Davie and Philip Larkin; the weekly review *Spectator* very much became a platform for this group of writers and poets. Undoubtedly we have here the processes of 'mediation' at work; though equally beyond doubt there really was a collectivity of like-minded poets very deliberately and explicitly reacting against the fashions of the forties. In 1955, one of them, D. J. Enright (b. 1920), an academic who spent most of his teaching career in such places as Japan and Egypt, produced an anthology *Poets of the 1950s*. A year later a further collection, *New Lines*, was presented by Robert Conquest (b. 1917), who, unusually in this company, had been through an upper-class education at Winchester as well as Magdalen College, Oxford: this collection contained nine poets (of whom six were academics): Conquest, Elizabeth Jennings (b. 1926), John Holloway (b. 1920), Larkin, Thom Gunn (b. 1929), Amis, Enright, Donald

Davie and Wain. Already, thanks to an October 1954 *Spectator* article entitled 'In the Movement', this group of poets had a name. In his Preface, Conquest set out what he took to be their objectives:

If one had briefly to distinguish the poetry of the fifties from its predecessors, I believe the most important general point would be that it submits to no great systems of theoretical constructs nor agglomeration of unconscious demands. It is free from both mystical and logical compulsions and — like modern philosophy — is empirical in its attitude to all that comes.

The main literary figures of the immediate post-war period had belonged to, in my definition, the upper class, apart from a few, as it were, fully licensed (mainly Celtic) bohemians. Members of 'The Movement' were educated at Oxford or Cambridge, but were generally from the lower ranges of the middle class, having moved upwards via grammar schools and scholarships. There was no consistency in political attitude or social criticism: here was an alternative cultural form to those which had dominated literature in the forties, but scarcely an alternative ideology. The Movement did not long remain a coherent movement: Davie and Gunn, in particular, moved towards American modernism.

Arguments over the existence, nature, and status of The Movement spluttered in the intellectual weeklies: developments in the novel and on the stage actually made it, in however distorted form, into the popular daily newspapers. The three key works were the first novel by Movement writer Kingsley Amis, *Lucky Jim* (published in January 1954), *Look Back in Anger*, by the unknown playwright John Osborne, presented at the Royal Court theatre on 8 May 1956, and *The Outsider* (published on 28 May 1956) by twenty-four-year-old unknown writer Colin Wilson, neither novel nor drama, but a quite erudite study of the quest of 'outsiders', mainly in literature, for a deeper understanding of life than is available to the mere multitudes. In the era prior to the building of the 'new universities' in the 1960s, the smaller English provincial universities had their origins in the early twentieth century; however, they

underwent considerable expansion under the educational policies of the post-war Labour governments. Perhaps it needed
Cambridge-educated eyes to spot the potential they offered as
the setting for a comic novel — the idea for what was to
become *Lucky Jim* came to Amis while visiting his friend Philip
Larkin, who was librarian at Leicester University. Jim Dixon,
newly appointed Assistant Lecturer in History, was lower-
middle-class in origins and tastes: the novel, in the fashion of
the Movement writers, mocks what Dixon sees as the elaborate
cultural pretensions of his boss, Professor Welch. Already Amis
was revealing his supreme ability to record accurately the things
people actually think and indeed sometimes say, rather than
what, by polite convention, they ought to think and say. *Lucky
Jim* was hailed across an amazingly wide cross-section of the
press as *the* novel representing the new writing of which only
connoisseurs of poetry had so far been properly aware.

Attention was then focused on John Wain's novel *Hurry On
Down*, which had actually been published, though not written,
several months before Amis's, and on the first novel by Oxford
philosophy don Iris Murdoch, *Under the Net*, which was published
a few months after *Lucky Jim*. *Hurry on Down* concerns a
lower-middle-class provincial figure, Joe Lumley, who moves
through a variety of jobs rather than take up the kind of upper-
middle-class employment available to him through his university
degree; though subsequently publishing *The Contenders*, in the
longer view Wain perhaps showed more consistent distinction
as a poet and a critic rather than as a novelist. With its manifest
naturalism, its narrator openly sharing his hesitations and doubts
with the reader, and its non-conforming, slightly bohemian
setting, *Under the Net* seemed to complete a neat trio: in fact
Murdoch was beginning the exploration, which she has continued ever since, of the likelihood that there is a 'non-naturalistic' world of the imagination below the 'net' of rational
organization believed in by philosophers from the Enlightenment to the nineteenth century. Some critics also now pointed
to an earlier novel, *Scenes from Provincial Life* (1950) by William
Cooper (pseudonym of H. S. Hoff) as the true precursor of
the 'new' novels whose characteristics were taken to be a hitherto unfashionable emphasis on the provincial and departures

from the manners conventionally associated with middle- and upper-middle-class life. Cooper's novel featured a cottage shared by two aspiring novelists, to which the narrator from time to time took his girlfriend, and his fellow novelist (also male) a boyfriend.

The mediatory role of press and critics is clear,[8] though beyond doubt Amis and Murdoch developed further into novelists of considerable stature. The brilliant, and utterly dedicated, theatrical director George Devine had founded the English Stage Company at the Royal Court theatre in order to try to present new plays which would break through the Rattigan-poetic drama-purely commercial and exploitative suffocation. It was Devine who gave Osborne his chance, and it was Devine who kept *Look Back in Anger* going, greatly assisted by a wildly enthusiastic *Observer* review by Kenneth Tynan, even though the play was not at that time paying its way commercially. Rather oddly, it was Colin Wilson's *The Outsider* that achieved overnight success (also assisted by an *Observer* review – by Philip Toynbee): Victor Gollancz had taken a personal liking to the book and thus marketed it as a general (rather than as a specialist) work, while another member of the firm had replaced Wilson's suggested title *The Pain Threshold* with the more arresting *The Outsider*. Most certainly, Wilson's book was based on impressively wide reading: while the critics praised his learning, journalists worked on the revelation that while working by day in the British Museum Wilson had been sleeping by night on Hampstead Heath. Then, almost by accident, the Royal Court press officer produced the notion that Osborne was 'a very angry young man'. 'Angry young men', particularly Wilson and Osborne (whose play now began to make serious money for the English Stage Company, as well as himself), but also the 'new' novelists and many associated with the Movement, became the centre of media attention.

Look Back in Anger is marvellous theatre, if often in a rather conventional way: act one opens with Jimmy Porter's upper-class wife, Alison, ironing his shirts; act two opens with Helena, the proud beauty, similarly employed. Throughout there is tremendous passion and vehemence. Jimmy Porter is certainly angry, as young men often are, as indeed most people sometimes can be at the tiniest irritations of life. Some of the apparently standard elements are there: a provincial setting; Jimmy Porter, though a university graduate, derives his living from running a sweet stall. Some of the anger, clearly of a class nature, is directed at Alison, her brother, her father, and their ilk, but most seems directed against the conventions and complacencies of society. There is certainly no coherent 'alternative ideology'; indeed Osborne attacked those who looked for profound meaning in the play's most famous line 'There aren't any good, brave causes left', explaining it as merely an expression of 'ordinary despair'.[9]

Of all the authors mentioned so far, only Wilson was genuinely working-class in social origins — his father worked in a Leicester boot and shoe factory, and he himself completed his formal education at the age of sixteen; but his book is the one most utterly lacking in social comment of any sort. Wilson's fame played an important part in creating the notion of the Angry Young man, but in itself it was short-lived; he left no legacy, and his later works were met with little but contempt. Osborne's play, however, not altogether devoid of clichés in itself, fully merits the cliché 'landmark'. Rude, exuberant plays, marking a thundering break with the era of Rattigan, became the staple of the English Stage Company at the Royal Court. Laurence Olivier, already being recognized as one of the greatest classical actors, expressed a wish to appear in·Osborne's next play, and so played Archie Rice, musical-hall entertainer in decline.

Opening on 10 April 1957, *The Entertainer* was again highly effective as drama: again, also, much generalized criticism is made of declining British society, but neither the play itself, nor what one knows about Osborne's intentions, fit the thesis that here was some kind of comprehensive condemnation of British imperialism in the aftermath of the Suez fiasco. Archie Rice is a memorable dramatic character, and *The Entertainer* is a more than worthy successor to *Look Back in Anger*; at the same time the involvement of a celebrity, Laurence Olivier, helped to ensure that the presentation of this play would be an important media event. But the press savaged Osborne's musical *The World of Paul Slickey*: this actually contained Osborne's sharpest and most sustained social criticism, directed at the world of newspapers, but in the Palace theatre (vast compared with the Royal Court) it was simply not possible to keep the play going beyond six weeks.

One further novel which the newspapers chose to associate with the Angry Young Man image is John Braine's *Room at the Top* (1957). In 1950 Braine had set himself up in London as a free-lance writer, a self-conscious 'intellectual', who wrote primarily to earn a living. Braine's father, as a child, had worked part-time in the Yorkshire woollen mills, but by the time of the birth in Bradford in 1922 of the future writer, he had moved into the lower-middle class as a sewage works supervisor; Braine's mother was a librarian. Already Braine was something of an outsider, since the family were Catholic. He left his Catholic grammar school at the age of sixteen, taking up various marginal white-collar jobs, ending up in the Bingley library. He served as a telegraphist in the Royal Navy between 1940 and 1943, before being invalided out with TB. Between 1952 and 1954 he had two further years with TB, encouraging him to concentrate on literary creation. Braine has said that the first seeds of the novel came when the sight of a rich man in an expensive car set him wondering how one achieved such a position. The novel is retrospective in mode, the rich man in the fifties looking back to the early post-war years. Joe Lampton (the narrator), son of a mill worker, having acquired an accountancy qualification while a prisoner of war in Germany, comes in 1947 from working-class Dufton to the Yorkshire city of Warley (modelled on Bradford) to take up a post in the City accountant's office under the Chief Accountant, Hoylake. He becomes involved both with Alice Aisgill, 'an older woman' married to a prosperous businessman, and with Susan Brown, daughter of the richest and most powerful man around, who is himself married to a member of the aristocracy. He ditches Alice to marry Susan and thus goes straight to 'the top'. Alice kills herself in a horrific car accident. The young Joe Lampton is fastidious and self-questioning, and has to be prodded by his friend Charles. The novel, then, concerns loss of innocence and the ambiguity and contradictions of different kinds of love: Joe does genuinely love Susan, towards whom he behaves fastidiously and protectively; his love for Alice, an experienced and self-confident woman with a perfectly decent husband, is a combination of friendship and profound sensuality, and his final parting from her takes place in a calm and matter-of-fact way.[10] There is also much on the material circumstances of post-war Britain, including some rather muted elements of social criticism. In sexual content the novel was not really more explicit than many that had been published earlier in the century, but it was down-to-earth and naturalistic, somewhat in the manner of William Cooper and Kingsley Amis, and it did deal bluntly with the realities of class and income differences. After five rejections, Braine's novel was accepted, against much internal opposition, by the respectable publishers Eyre and Spottiswood. On publication in March 1957, it was immediately recognized as being in the school of Amis and Osborne: 'If you want to know the way in which the young products of the Welfare State are feeling and reacting,' wrote Richard Lester in the *Evening Standard*, '*Room at the Top* will tell you.' Hard cover sales amounted to 34,000 (greatly assisted by a mention on the BBC TV programme *Panorama*), there was serialization in the *Daily Express* and a Book Club edition sold 125,000; Penguin Books offered for the paperback rights on 7 May, and the deal was concluded by 15 May 1957.

The Movement was dead, but it had expressed a coherent point of view, and its most distinguished member, Philip Larkin, consolidated a reputation as one of the most distinguished English poets of the late twentieth century; the Angry Young Man had always been something of a media invention, but beneath the fantasy there were genuine stirrings in British culture: the full force of these only emerge in our second period of study with, for a start, the transformed *Room at the Top* of the film version.

But altogether different developments were proceeding at the same time. The very opulence and foreignness to which the Movement had objected were lusciously celebrated in the novels making up Lawrence Durrell's *Alexandria Quartet*: with the sort of pretentiousness which Amis personally delighted in exploding, Durrell spoke of his 'relativity proposition', which turned out to mean no more than presenting the same situations from the different points of view of different participants in the novel (something Joyce Cary, for instance, had already done very effectively, though without the opulent language). Nothing could be less provincial than the settings of the novels by the most acclaimed new 'serious' writer of the 1950s, William Golding (b. 1911), who wrote deceptively naturalistic works about deeply unnatural situations, which in fact turned out to be highly symbolic fables about the presence of evil and the difficulties of achieving good. Golding, after a respectable grammar school and Oxford education, war service in the Royal Navy, and many years as a schoolmaster with a theatrical bent, came late to novel-writing: he is the epitome of the writer with a serious moral purpose, the production and consumption of his books little affected by contemporary fashion and commercial considerations. *Lord of the Flies* (1954) is the deity which a group of school children, shipwrecked on a deserted island, come to worship as they regress towards a very primitive, very cruel, hierarchical form of tribal society. *Pincher Martin* (1955) has a seaman shipwrecked on a rock where he struggles desperately for survival; save that, in one of the most powerfully shocking endings provided by any novel of the time; it turns out that Pincher Martin has been dead all along, so that his struggles to justify himself must have been taking place in after-life. *The Inheritors* (1956) shows early man brutally establishing society and exterminating his gentler Neanderthal ancestors. Golding is very much a novelist of the twentieth century, deeply aware of man's inhumanity to man. Later he was to be canonized by the educational system (yet another form of 'mediation') which selected *Lord of the Flies* as a standard literary text for contemporary English literature; Golding, also, was recognized by the critics as part of the efflorescence of novel writing more generally associated with Amis, Murdoch and Wain (though, of course, he had absolutely nothing in common with the first and third of these): but it remains difficult − and, indeed, I would say wrong − to find any neat social explanation for the emergence of William Golding.

Foreign influences were directly exercised through drama. Translations of Jean Anouilh enjoyed West End success; there were more specialized audiences for Sartre and Brecht. In the longer view the most important event of the fifties in the development of British drama was the presentation in 1955 of the English translation of a play by the expatriate Irishman Samuel Beckett (b. 1906), who wrote in French. This was *Waiting for Godot*, a play which *seems* to consist only of the conversations of two tramps about a third character who never appears, and to which the convenient label usually applied is the slightly unsatisfactory one of 'Theatre of the Absurd'. For the period covered by this book Beckett was both the most innovative and truly modernist dramatist (*Endgame*, 1958; *Krapp's Last Tape*, 1958; *Happy Days*, 1961 – all presented at the Royal Court). Beckett asks, in effect, whether at any time life is worth having, and he presents this not as a question for debate (which would be pointless), but as a permanent doubt. His influence on British theatre was immense: he was not himself, of course, British.

Writers catering to an easy market there were, of course, aplenty. Agatha Christie (1890–1976) continued to produce formulae detective stories, cunningly contrived to keep the reader guessing to the end, but utterly without literary merit (though praised by Labour prime minister Clement Attlee whose early literary sensibilities were now concealed in a deliberate man-of-the-people stance). Enormous commercial success continued to be enjoyed by C. S. Forester (1899–1966), featuring the exploits of Horatio Hornblower in the Napoleonic wars. It was in the fifties, as the cheap lending libraries (often attached to ordinary shops) went into terminal decline, that the publishing firm of Mills and Boon began their colossally successful paperback ventures in the marketing of light romances. It was often said that much of the most blatant exploitation literature, featuring private detectives, sex and violence, came from America. However, against the popularity of, say, Hank Jansen one can set that of Peter Cheyney, who was English to the core, and had his characters speak the weirdest kind of pidgin American. At the same time the fifties marked an important stage in the contemporary development whereby certain fictional genres (for example, crime stories, spy stories and science fiction) are no longer snobbishly rejected as unsuitable for serious treatment. An important precursor of what became known in the sixties as the new wave in science fiction was John Wyndham (pseudonym of John Harris, 1903–69), with his *The Day of the Triffids* (1951), *The Craken Wakes* (1953) and *The Middwich Cuckoos* (1957).

Notes

1 Edward Lucie-Smith (ed.), *British Poetry since 1945* (1985), p. 79.
2 Ibid., p. 72.
3 Ibid., p. 95.
4 Stevie Smith, 'Tenuous and Precarious', printed in Lucie-Smith, *British Poetry*, pp. 109–10.
5 Evelyn Waugh, *Sword of Honour* (1952–62, 1964 edn), p. 266.
6 See Ronald Hayman, *The Set-Up*: *An Anatomy of the English Theatre Today* (1973), p. 119.
7 Kenneth Tynam, *He that plays the King* (1950), p. 142.
8 On this issue Harry Ritchie's meticulous study, *Success Stories: Literature and the Media in England 1950–1959* (1988) is highly illuminating. The standard work is *The Movement* (1980) by Blake Morrison.
9 John Osborne in Tom Maschler, *Declaration* (1957).
10 Readers' views may well have been coloured by the subsequent film, which I discuss in part II: detailed references to the novel can be found in my chapter '*Room at the Top*: the Novel and the Film' in Arthur Marwick (ed.), *The Arts, Literature and Society* (1990), ch. 9.

4 Music, Painting and Sculpture: Modest Openings to the World

Music

Any consideration of music at once draws attention to the distinction between 'culture in Britain' and 'British culture', the basic product for consumption in concert halls and opera houses continuing to be the classics of Beethoven, Brahms, Mozart, Verdi, Wagner etc. Musical production and consumption are very markedly affected by technology: a critical development at the beginning of the fifties was the invention and sale of the long-playing gramophone record inducing new levels of expectation among listeners. Prior to that, in the organization of entrepreneurship and, indeed, in the very shape of the buildings in which music was played, the Second World War had had some important consequences. During the war the Sadler's Wells Opera and the Sadler's Wells Ballet were forced out on tour through the benighted provinces. At the end of the war the Sadler's Wells theatre was reopened as the home exclusively of English-language opera, while the Sadler's Wells Ballet (becoming the Royal Ballet) transferred to the Royal Opera House, Covent Garden, which from being a commercial venue playing host to visits by the top international operatic companies, was re-established, with Arts Council support, as a national home for opera and ballet. During the war, to the outrage of opera lovers, it had been used as a commercial dance hall, much patronized by servicemen. The gala opening performance in February 1946 by the long-established ballet company was of *The Sleeping Beauty*, by the Russian, Tchaikovsky. It took time to build up an opera company: the gala opening did not take place till January 1947, the opera being *Carmen*, by the Frenchman, Bizet. Music at least was not parochial, though it might be argued that a neglect of British composers was a parochial British characteristic. Opera, self-evidently, commanded a smaller audience than drama; on the whole, it was an audience drawn from higher up the social scale. Covent Garden, in its more expensive seats, was a social focus for the upper class and upper-middle class. Sadler's Wells, with its opera in translation and regular provincial tours, was much more a resort for the middle class and lower-middle class. Since 1934 there had existed what was almost a paradigmatic upper-class institution, the Glyndebourne Opera House on the Sussex Downs.

But let us pursue the theme of the effects of war as both destruction and affirmation. The Queen's Hall in London was destroyed for ever, the Free Trade Hall, home of Manchester's famous Hallé orchestra, was not fit for reoccupation until 1951. The Royal Liverpool Philharmonic and the Hallé became full-time permanent orchestras for the first time in 1942 and 1943 respectively. In 1944 the City of Birmingham Orchestra was reformed; and at the end of the war the four major London orchestras – the Royal Philharmonic (brought together again in 1946 under the direction of Sir Thomas Beecham), the London Symphony, the London Philharmonic, and the Philharmonia – were re-established as self-governing institutions. Developments in the post-war years were the reorganization of the Scottish Orchestra into the permanent Scottish National Orchestra in 1950, and the expansion under Charles Groves of the Bournemouth Symphony Orchestra in 1954. But without doubt the major force in British music was the BBC – through its own Symphony Orchestra, through its regional orchestras, through its broadcasts on the new post-war Third Programme, through its sponsorship each summer of the Royal Albert Hall Promenade Concerts (the Proms), and through the valuable subventions it offered each time it broadcast a concert or music festival. The war experience had given a considerable boost to the notion of state and civic sponsorship of various social services. The Arts Council, formed out of the wartime CEMA, became an important channel of government subsidy towards music and the other arts. The grandest civic venture was the launching in 1947 of the Edinburgh International Festival of Music and Drama, to plans conceived by Rudolf Byng, general manager of the Glyndebourne Opera, Harvey Wood, director of the British Council in Scotland, and Sir John Faulkner, Lord Provost of Edinburgh. In 1948, under the inspiration of Benjamin Britten (1913–76), the Aldeborough Festival on the Suffolk coast was founded.

Britten, indeed, was the brightest star among the younger composers, in a scene where musicians who had made their names in the inter-war years, particularly William Walton, and, above all, Ralph Vaughan Williams, were still very dominating figures. Though sensitive to modernistic innovations in musical language, neither went anything like as far as leading continental contemporaries. In the thirties Britten had been a bright young intellectual, associated with the group that looked to W. H. Auden for leadership. Despairing of British society, Britten, together with his close friend, the tenor Peter Pears, left for America in August 1939. However, though pacifists, they were not deserters, and in early 1942 they voluntarily returned to embattled Britain to submit themselves to the call-up process: they were in fact given exemption from military service on condition that they gave recitals for CEMA. Much of Britten's creative energies were devoted to composing an opera based on a poem by George Crabbe: as conscientious objectors, and therefore to a degree outsiders, Britten and Pears identified with the strangely independent and stubborn character of Peter Grimes. If the founding of the Edinburgh International Festival is one impressive testimonial to the new spirit of internationalism, sanity, and reconciliation released by the war, the fact that it was Britten's opera *Peter Grimes* which was chosen to reopen the Sadler's Wells theatre on 7 June 1945 was another. In discussing works of art it is important to remember the personal, as well as the political and social: Paul Griffiths suggests 'that Grimes the outcast, acutely sensitive but profoundly understood, was a projection of Britten's own feelings as a homosexual in a society where homosexual expression was strongly repressed, or perhaps, more profoundly, of his feelings as a personality which censored a vital part of itself.' Griffiths, discussing Britten's musical language, then continues:

If so, then his divided self would have found an echo in the divided nature of the tonal language in his time. No composer after Schoenberg's break into atonality could use major-minor harmony in entire security that this was the natural, inevitable language of music; there had to be a degree of irony. In early Britten, in works like Bridge Variations, this had been expressed as parody, but in *Peter Grimes* and most later works, it becomes rather an awareness of a fall from a musical state of grace. The yearning sevenths of Grimes's part are emblems of a yearning for the pure harmony of an earlier stage in musical history.[1]

After *Peter Grimes* most of Britten's operas were conceived of as small-scale chamber operas: *The Rape of Lucretia* (1946), requiring only soloists and an orchestra of twelve, provided the impetus for the formation of the English Opera Group, for whom Britten wrote his other small-scale operas, including *Albert Herring* (1947 — a comic opera) and *The Turn of the Screw* (1954 — based on the Henry James short story, and his first major use of some of the ideas of twelve-note serialism).

The tension between personal inclination and the demands of musical entrepreneurship can be seen in the two operas, *Billy Budd* and *Gloriana*, which *had* to be on a lavish scale: both were commissioned by Covent Garden, the first for the Festival of Britain and the second for the Coronation of Elizabeth II.

Where Britten was a child prodigy, Michael Tippett (b. 1909) was a late developer. Unlike Britten also, Tippett suffered imprisonment for his refusal to undertake military service. He was known in 1945 only for his oratorio *A Child of our Time*, one of a handful of works ranking with Elgar's *The Spirit of England* (1916—17), Shostakovich's *Leningrad Symphony* (1941), and Britten's later *A War Requiem* (1956—61) which are public statements in music about war: the 'Child of our Time' is a Jewish boy who, through shooting a Nazi diplomat in Paris, unwittingly unleashes a new spate of persecution upon his people. In 1946 Tippett began the composition of the opera

The Midsummer Marriage, which was not completed till 1952. By that time

this restatement of Shakespearean (*A Midsummer Nights Dream*) and Mozartian (*The Magic Flute*) themes had acquired a range of reference that embraced the dream plays of Yeats and Shaw, the later poetry of Eliot, a vision of the human psyche taken from Jung, the previously acquired musical synthesis of seventeenth-century English and contemporary European styles, blues, and a new bounding movement that could keep its propulsive energy even through musical texture alive with decoration.[2]

There followed the *Fantasia Concertante* on the theme of Correlli for string orchestra (1953), the piano concerto (1953—5) and the second symphony (1956—7). The first performance of *The Midsummer Marriage* took place in 1955, in a production designed by the distinguished sculptor Barbara Hepworth. Tippett did not in this period receive wide acclaim; how acclaim came to him, as with how Britten came to present his greatest work, form part of another, and rather more exhilarating, episode in British cultural history.

Ballet has had an erratic history in Britain. The challenge during the war of touring the provinces, and temporary occupation of the New Theatre in London, actually enhanced standards at the Sadler's Wells ballet and Margot Fonteyn (b. 1919) emerged as a ballerina of undisputable world class. As the popularity of ballet continued to increase in the post-war years, a number of new companies were founded: the Festival Ballet in London, Scottish Ballet in Glasgow and the Northern Ballet Theatre in Manchester. Britain had a world class choreographer in Frederick Ashton who continued to build on his considerable achievements of the pre-war years.

Painting and sculpture

Painting needs neither translation, nor a vast orchestra; on the other hand much effort and planning are required for the mounting of large exhibitions, especially international ones, which, almost inevitably, will be one-off events. Most influential were the Matisse—Picasso exhibition held at the Victoria and Albert Museum in the winter of 1945—6, and the exhibition mounted ten years later entitled *Modern Art in the United States*, which culminated in examples of Abstract Expressionism. Another important exhibition, indicating that foreignness was not always synonymous with the most advanced modernism, was the Arts Council Tate Gallery exhibition of 1955, *Four French Realists*. Important domestic influences were the art schools, where one single teacher could often be very influential, and, of course, the commercial dealers: for example, figurative art was positively promoted by the dealer Henry Rowland and by Helen Lessore, proprietor of the Beaux-Arts Gallery (of this gallery, the artist John Bratby most unkindly recalled, it 'was a dry and unhappy place, concerned not with the joy of life and its presentation in oils, but with the misery of the soul, Angst, the Human Predicament, Man's Condition, ugliness and truth'.[3]) Whether the various 'schools' or 'groups' should be seen as helping to form art, or whether it is the art that forms the schools, is a moot point.

No single 'ism' predominates in post-war British art (does it ever anywhere?), while, of course, several 'isms' can coexist in one painting. The effects of the war experience had been to intensify a very clearly identifiable Britishness, most usually shelved under the convenient but not very communicative label, 'neo-Romanticism' — as seen, for instance, in the watercolours of bomb-damaged buildings by John Piper, paintings which work both as romantic statements and beautiful abstract designs. The great international collection in the National Gallery had been transferred to relative safety in Wales, while the Tate Gallery was seriously affected by bomb damage: however the interest in Britishness and British artists was such that when an exhibition of works by younger British artists, organized by the Tate, was held at the National Gallery, the crowds were so large that the police had to be brought in. The ending of war, however, brought, in part at least, an emphasis on opening up to international influences.

In the inter-war years the flag of abstraction had been flown vigorously by Ben Nicholson. On the world scene, and particularly in the United States, abstract art, the target of both Hitlerism and Stalinism, became associated with notions of democratic and capitalist freedoms. Probably this is not a notion to be pushed too hard as far as British painters were concerned, though it is true that of the three abstract painters who formed the St Ives School in Cornwall, one, Naum Gabo (1890–1977, born in Russia, and best known as a 'Constructivist' sculptor), did leave for the United States in 1946; the other two were Ben Nicholson (1894–1982) and Barbara Hepworth (1903–75). After the war this 'school' was reinforced by the association with it of Patrick Heron (b. 1920) and Alan Davie (b. 1920). The St Ives School is best known for its abstract landscapes, loosely, but more emotionally than topographically, based on Cornish scenes. Davie, it may be noted, was a Scot, and product of the Edinburgh College of Art, an important innovative influence, particularly later under the directorship of Robin Philipson. A form of Abstract Expressionism, therefore, was being produced by some British artists before the great American exhibition of 1956 which, certainly, did have a tremendous impact on Patrick Heron; Heron, however, then reacted quite strongly against it.

The earlier work of Victor Pasmore had shown representational and romantic elements. He was directly affected by the Picasso and Matisse exhibition, confessing to being 'very much moved' by the work of Picasso, 'even though I didn't like it'. By 1947 Pasmore had reached the position that 'abstraction is a logical culmination of paintings since the Renaissance'.[4] Pasmore moved on to making constructions out of plywood and plastic and thus is associated with a group called the Constructionists who claimed to be engaged on a 'search for a constructive, not just an imitative reality'.[5] Expressionism, art which contains strong representational elements, but with 'unnatural' colour and distortions so as to heighten emotional expression, had its representative in David Bomberg (1890–1957), who taught part-time at the Borough Polytechnic, just south of the River Thames. He gave inspiration to the Borough group (1947–50) and the Borough Bottega (1953–6), whose leading figures were Frank Auerbach (b. Berlin, 1931) and Leon Kossoff (b. 1926) – who ever since have held a special place in British art for their atmospheric representations of London in its many guises.

Some of the most outstanding painters of the time, with their highly individualistic talents and modes of expression, particularly Francis Bacon (b. 1909) and Lucien Freud (grandson of Sigmund, he had arrived in Britain in 1933), are sometimes loosely grouped together as the 'School of London', which had its base in the Colony Room, a drinking den in Dean Street, Soho. Freud was already known for his distinctive and expressive nudes; Bacon, descended from a well-connected family of the Anglo-Irish ascendancy (he was a collateral descendent of his illustrious Elizabethan namesake), had been excused war service because of his asthma, but did not show anything between 1937 and 1945. Completely untrained, he had made sporadic attempts to set himself up as a painter. An exhibition at the Lefevre Gallery in April 1945, which contained works by such better-known British artists as Matthew Smith and Henry Moore, also included a large triptych by Bacon entitled *Three Studies for Figures at the Base of a Crucifixion* (Plate 1): this contained those ingredients by which Bacon was eventually to become well known — malignant, ominous, twisted figures, part-human, part-animal. From most critics the response was one of outrage and ridicule. But the sheer power of his work — Bacon spoke of making 'the paint speak louder than the story — quickly brought paintings first attacked as being obsessive, ferocious distortions into the front line of critical acclaim. Frances Spalding suggests that, 'to a post-war audience, these ghoulish celebrants of murderous acts were a horrific reminder of human bestiality'.[6] Against that, one must put Bacon's own statement that he had 'nothing to say about the human condition'.[7] Bacon has also spoken of his aim to 'unlock the valves of feeling and therefore return the onlooker to life more violently'. In his later interviews with the art critic David Sylvester, Bacon gave an interesting account of how he came to do a major work in 1946:

One of the pictures I did in 1946, the one like a butcher's shop, came to me as an accident. I was attempting to make a bird alighting on a field. And it may have been bound up with the three forms that had

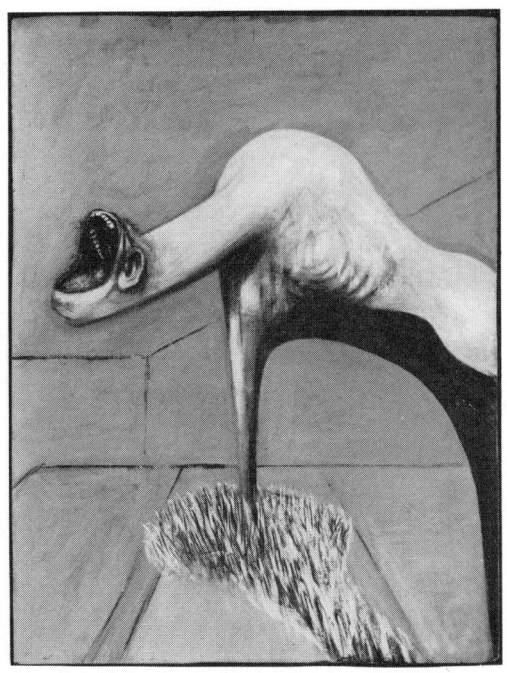

Plate 1 Francis Bacon, *Three Studies for Figures at the Base of a Crucifixion* (c. 1944). Oil on board. Each 940 × 737 mm. Acknowledgments to the artist and the Tate Gallery.

gone before ['Three studies for figures at a base of a crucifixion', to which I have already referred], but suddenly the lines that I had drawn suggested something totally different, and out of this suggestion arose this picture. I had no intention to do this picture, I never thought of it that way. It was like one continuous accident mounting on top of another.[8]

Like an overwhelming number of the producers of art of all kinds in this period, Bacon and Freud came from the upper reaches of society. However, both Robert Colquohoun (1914–62) and Robert MacBryde (1913–66) had emerged from the West of Scotland working class. Both were already manifestly influenced by Picasso and Braque, but derived new energies from the Picasso–Matisse exhibition. MacBryde and Colquohoun belonged to the hard-drinking bohemia of Dylan

Thomas, the world against which The Movement saw itself as rebelling; like the Welsh poet they both drank themselves to death.

A very conscious looking to 'abroad' can be found in Graham Sutherland, who from 1947 spent several months of each year in the South of France, clearly seeing himself as standing in an international, rather than a purely British tradition. 'In his post-1945 work . . .

Sutherland refashions nature, transforming rocks into womb-like conglomerates, thornbushes into crucifixions or a crown of thorns. Often situated within an indeterminate space, his writhing forms create knots of interest, like small stings of hate. A similar undercurrent of brutality can be discovered in his portraiture, in the harsh characterisation which, once the initial affront has worn off, is subtly flattering.[9]

More than, say, Bacon or the two Scots, Sutherland depended upon traditional forms of patronage, both ecclesiastical and lay. For St Matthew's Church, Northampton, he painted a crucifixion, and for the new Coventry Cathedral, between 1954 and 1957 he designed the tapestry 'Christ in Glory in the Tetramorph'; for Somerset Maugham, Lord Beaverbrook and the Honorable Edward Sackville-West he painted what were to become well-known portraits (Churchill never found *his* portrait 'flattering', not even 'subtly'!). Other artists tended to be more dependent on the private galleries; John Piper drew a good deal of his income from the reproductions made of his water colours.

In England, the new artistic movement which drew attention of a rather similar kind to that attracted by The Movement and the Angry Young men was that associated with certain provincial (key word!) artists: John Bratby (b. 1928), Jack Smith (b. 1928 in Sheffield) and Edward Middleditch (b. 1923). To this group the art critic David Sylvester in 1954 gave the name the 'Kitchen Sink School', the phrase then sometimes being applied to such dramatists as Arnold Wesker (discussed in part II of this book). This movement drew further inspiration from the French Realists whose exhibition at the Tate in 1955 I have already mentioned; it was supported, as I have also mentioned, by such entrepreneurs as Henry Rowland and Helen Lessore. In addition it had the initial support of the influential Marxist art critic and novelist John Berger, who sponsored 'Looking Forward' exhibitions at the Whitechapel Art Gallery, in working-class East London, in 1952, 1953 and 1956. Berger, however, regressed towards fundamentalism, beginning to pose the question: 'Does this work of art help or encourage men to know and claim their social rights?'[10]

The question of a distinctive 'Scottishness' comes up in interesting form with Joan Eardley (1912–65), whose English officer father met her Scottish mother in Glasgow during the First World War. She was born in Sussex, but studied at the Glasgow Art School, thereafter being thoroughly identified with the Scottish art world, its 'colourist' and 'expressionist' traditions (well represented by Anne Redpath and Henderson Blyth). Eardley showed her devotion to life and to art by herself living in a Glasgow slum tenement while she did her expressive paintings of the local urchins; in 1956 she moved to Catterline in North East Scotland where she concentrated mainly on expressionist landscapes.[11]

It is sculpture more than any other art form which betrays an almost incestuous internal process of successive rebellions against the older generation. Against the monumental human carvings of Henry Moore (1898–1986, his work only achieved international renown after 1945), Reg Butler (1913–81), Lynn Chadwick (b. 1914) and Michael Ayrton (1921–75) produced works which were modelled or welded. The influence of the Italian Giacometti is apparent (though till 1955, when his first retrospective was held, entirely based on photographs). Butler in 1952 won the competition for a design for *The Political Prisoner* (the sculpture itself was never built).

The whole question of the 'pop revolution' is a leading topic in part II of this book. There is, as I have already said, validity in the division between popular and élite culture, though this should never be seen as utterly rigid. The group of painters I am now going to look at in concluding this chapter offer bridges both forwards to the great artistic transformations of the 1960s and, as it were, laterally to the popular modes of industrial and commercial design and advertising. As so often,

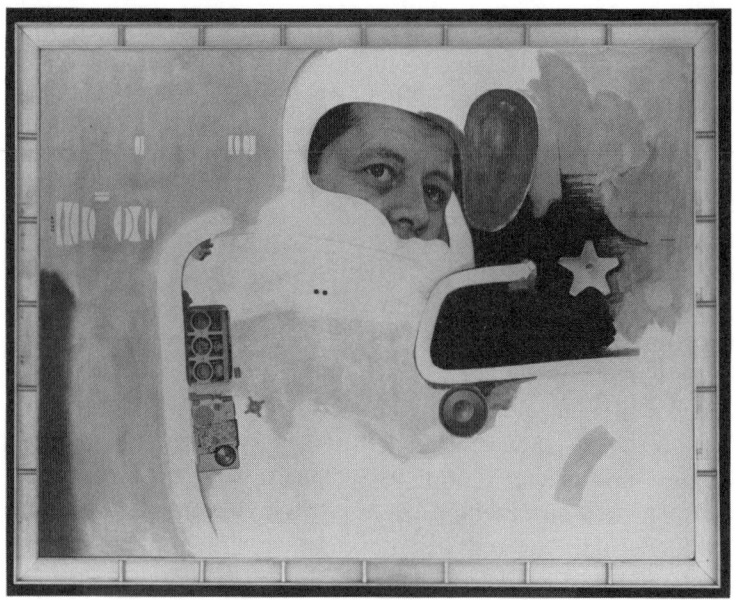

Plate 2   Richard Hamilton, *Towards a Definitive Statement on the Coming Trends in Men's Wear and Accessories: (a) together let us explore the stars* (1962). Oil and collage on wood. 610 × 813 mm. Acknowledgements to the artist, the Design and Artists Copyright Society Ltd, and the Tate Gallery.

Frances Spalding hits the nail on the head, when she points out that the Pop Art of the fifties 'never surrendered its fine art status': Richard Hamilton (b. 1922) delighted in 'authorial intrusion'[12] – a phrase nicely fitted to the difficult task of distinguishing high art from lesser art. It should be added, however, that the art critic Lawrence Alloway declared that the pop artists should abolish the distinctions between 'high' and 'low' art and instead talk of a 'fine/pop art continuum'.[13]

In 1952 the Independent Group, whose two main pre-occupations were modern technology and mass-media culture, began meeting at the Institute of Contemporary Arts (ICA). This group included artist and sculptor Eduardo Paolozzi (b. 1924), architectural historian, critic and journalist, Reyner Banham, Lawrence Alloway, and the architects Peter and Alison Smithson. The Independent Group organized an exhibition in

1956 entitled 'This is Tomorrow'. Hamilton produced the painting *Just what is it that makes today's homes so different, so appealing?* (1956), not reproduced, but see Plate 2) in order that it could be reproduced as a catalogue illustration and poster for the exhibition. It is not inaccurate to think of this painting, with its clever references to the technology and mass-media culture of the time, and this exhibition as marking the real beginning of the Pop Art movement in Britain. The three artists associated with the second wave of Pop Art were all students at the Royal College of Art during the mid fifties: Peter Blake (b. 1932), the title of whose *Children Reading Comics* (1954) says much about the subject matter of this art form, Joe Tilson (b. 1938) and Richard Smith (b. 1931), who subsequently turned towards more abstract art.

The pretensions of Pop Art to high art status were bolstered by continental art theory which placed it in the tradition of Dada and Surrealism and by the writings of French structuralists Levi-Strauss and Roland Barthes, who valued the naive as a window on the subconscious.

Notes

1 Paul Griffiths, 'Music', in *The Cambridge Guide to the Arts in Britain: Since the Second World War* (ed. Boris Ford, 1988), p. 56.
2 Ibid., p. 61.
3 Quoted by Frances Spalding, *British Art since 1900* (1986), p. 162.
4 Sir John Rothenstein, *Modern English Painting: Wood to Hockney* (1974), p. 151.
5 Spalding, *British Art*, p. 175.
6 Ibid., p. 146.
7 Quoted by Spalding, ibid., p. 149.
8 David Sylvester, *The Brutality of Fact: Interviews with Francis Bacon* (3rd edn, 1987), p. 11.
9 Spalding, *British Art*, p. 152.
10 Ibid., p. 161.
11 See William Buchanan, *Joan Eardley* (1976).
12 Spalding, *British Art*, p. 192.
13 Ibid.

5 Rebuilding and Redesigning Britain

Writing in 1973, Charles Jencks declared recent British architecture 'a battle field ... saturated with the shell holes of polemic'.[1] Sixteen years later the polemic, if anything, had intensified, with the Prince of Wales leading the attack on modern architecture, architects responding that, for mistakes made, politicians not architects were to blame. Inevitably, I shall in this chapter wish to raise questions of when (the forties, the fifties, later?) and why the major errors were initiated; but I shall try also to restore a contemporary perspective, stressing that at the time the squabbles were almost entirely within the architectural profession, the wholesale denunciation of planners, developers and architects not coming till the later sixties.

First let us remind ourselves that the habit of flattening existing buildings in order to put up new ones is as old as civilization itself: we all know about the Victorians, but for replacing the beautiful (particularly Georgian houses) with the boring and the banal, private and public builders of the 1930s have much to answer for. A number of forces, some of them contradictory, governed architectural production in the post-war years. War damage to the built environment was considerable (though, as contemporary photographs show, neither the Elephant and Castle in London nor the Bull Ring in Birmingham, subsequently horrendous victims of redevelopment, was irredeemably damaged): the greatest need and most urgent concern of the electorate was housing. With a government committed to public initiatives and public control it was not surprising that there was a marked movement of architects from private practice to public service, a net swing of 40 per cent among members of the Royal Institute of British Architects (RIBA) by 1948. There was a very lively younger generation centred on the Modern Architectural Research Group (MARS) founded in 1933, and publishing their theories in the *Architectural Review*. Sympathetic to the ideals of the Labour government, they were also very much under the spell of Le Corbusier and his notion of massive 'Habitational units', elevating family life to the level of public monuments. The younger architects (around forty years of age at the end of the war) made remarkable progress, gaining seven out of ten places on the RIBA council in 1950. Publication in the late forties of Mies van der Rohe's designs for the Illinois Institution of Technology brought a further influence from one of the international giants of modernism.[2] But encompassing all the pressures, all the theories, all the ideals was Britain's fundamental shortage of cash (the development, to meet the needs of war, of industrial building techniques being only tiny compensation).

The main emphasis to the mid fifties was on building houses and schools, Aneurin Bevan, Minister of Health, insisting that with respect to their amenities at least, all houses should be built to high standards. Their style was what Reyner Banham called 'People's Detailing', described by Charles Jencks as 'the English version of Socialist realism': 'pitched roofs, bricky materials, ticky-tacky, cute latticework, little nooks and crannies, pictures profiles all snuggled within a cardboard like rectitude'.[3] The first generation of new towns, started in the forties, also catered to the traditional taste for low-rise housing set in a reasonable space, while at the same time adopting some of the tenets of the International functionalist style. Harlow (planned by an active modernist of the thirties, Frederick Gibberd) has been widely praised, though it also quickly manifested a problem which became endemic in post-war architecture: the smart white terraces in the International style by two other young modernists, Maxwell Fry and Jane Drew, simply wore much less well than some of their more traditional brick-built neighbours.

Industrial techniques for building schools were pioneered in

Hertfordshire, then, in 1948, taken up by Ministry of Education. Several of these schools won international reputations, for instance, the Henry Hartland Grammar School at Worksop, a secondary modern school at Wokingham, a primary school at Amersham, and a village school at Finmere in Oxfordshire, all light and airy, not especially impressive from the outside, but extremely well designed in their use of space inside. Major public building was less successful. Government regulations limited building volume (and therefore height) by plot area: thus such public buildings as did begin to go up, the most notorious example being the Shell Centre on London's South Bank, were not only oppressively boring, but often had an ungainly squat appearance.

For the out-and-out modernists more scope seemed to offer itself as the local authorities in the big cities decided that lengthy housing lists and shortages of urban land could only be overcome through building multi-storey housing estates. Quarry Hill in Leeds was still seen as a model of socialist planning, though the standard most admired was that which had been set in the pre-war years by the private firm of Tecton, builders of the celebrated North London tower blocks, Highpoint One and Two in Highgate (designed by Berthold Lubetkin) — upper-middle class accommodation of almost American opulence. Similar blocks, designed for working-class accommodation, were commissioned from the famous building engineers Ove Arup, to be built in less fashionable Finsbury. This was followed by the multi-storey estate Churchill Gardens, built at Pimlico to accommodate 5,000 people, by the more avant-garde firm of Powell and Moya, and the Wholefield estate, Paddington, West London, where the influence of perhaps the most inspired of the younger generation, Denys Lasdun, was apparent. From 1950, public housing in London became the direct responsibility of the London County Council (LCC) architectural department. Now, in effect, the architects *were* the politicians. In its day (1952—9), though, the department's realization at Roehampton in South West London, of the Le Corbusier vision of a high-rise city set in a park was lauded as one of the great achievements of contemporary architecture.

The first great break from the needs of home, family and

children towards the need for public spectacle came with the preparation of the bombed-out South Bank site for the 1951 Festival of Britain. It was actually during the war that the Royal Society of Arts, sharing in the spirit of the time, proposed a new Great Exhibition, to echo that of 1851. After the war the cry was taken up by liberal-minded newspaper editor Gerald Barry, persuading the Labour government of the appropriateness of celebrating the new world of reconstruction. Appointed director of architecture, Hugh Casson designed the entire exhibition area in the modernist idiom of a single concept linking together spaces and buildings: the major temporary constructions were the Dome of Discovery, designed by Ralph Tubbs, and the Skylon designed by J. H. Moya. The Royal Festival Hall was really a London County Council project, designed by their chief architect, Robert Matthew, and would have been built anyway, festival or no festival.

The precise significance of the Festival of Britain has been much argued over. It seems clear that it did have a powerful effect in spreading what was conceived to be a 'modern' style in architecture; whether this was good or bad, and whether because too modern, or not modern enough, has formed the basis of debate. Equally, thanks to the opportunity the festival offered to the Council for Industrial Design, interior design was greatly influenced. Though there was a travelling festival exhibition which visited Manchester, Leeds, Birmingham and Notthingham, and quite a number of smaller individual festival efforts, as well as some larger ones, such as the Exhibition of Industrial Power in Glasgow, the Festival of Britain in reality, if not intention, came over as very much a metropolitan affair. However, Reyner Banham has stressed the coincident expansion in the mass media: 'If the Festival was not a "turning point in taste" itself,' he wrote, 'it was part of the raw material that fed the influence that did help to modernise public taste: the media.'[4]

Many of the new housing estates of the post-war years – and most of the occupants were probably glad of it – were very traditional in style. How the houses were furnished depended on a number of factors. Wartime necessity had led to the creation of 'utility' furniture – one nationwide economical style; wartime aspiration had led to the creation of the Council for Industrial Design. Both of those upper-class socialists Hugh Dalton, president of the Board of Trade during the war, and Sir Stafford Cripps, his successor in the Labour government after 1945, were enthusiastic supporters of good design. Cripps played an important part in the presentation of the 1946 Design Exhibition at the Victoria and Albert Museum, 'Britain Can Make It'. A million-and-a-half people visited this exhibition of simple, unfussy, rational products, each a tribute to the best in modern functionalism. Unfortunately, few were available for general sale, so that the exhibition was quickly nicknamed 'Britain Can't Have It'. In 1948 reform was carried through at the Royal College of Art: the theories were those of the great German centre of rational design of the 1920s, the *Bauhaus*, but the practice was very much that of the progressive element in the British upper class, as in so many of the other experiments of the post-1945 period. The Council for Industrial Design worked hard to cash in on the popularization of good contemporary design achieved by the Festival of Britain. In 1956 the Design Centre was opened in Haymarket, London, and a year later the Design Centre awards began. Gradually manufacturers were persuaded that it was worth trying to attain the label 'Design Centre approved'. Yet, as Fiona MacCarthy has remarked — and how typical this is of the entire British cultural scene — 'Design was still in many ways an amiable clique. Identical professors seemed forever giving prizes to their own RCA students, identical designers were forever smiling thanks to the Duke of Edinburgh.'[5] Much British design was in fact highly derivative, with Scandinavian influences heavily in evidence in the fifties.

As we saw in the previous chapter, design and 'high art' were seen as coming together by the Pop Art enthusiasts of the Independent Group, among whom were the architects Alison and Peter Smithson. The Smithsons were responsible for Hunstanton School, Norfolk (1950–4), an attempt to apply the ideas of both Mies van der Rohe and Le Corbusier, and widely taken as the first example of what was called the New Brutalism. In a 1954 article with that title, the *Architect's Journal* declared:

in that this building seems often to ignore the children for which it is built, it is hard to define it as *architecture* at all. It is a formalist structure which will please only the architects, and a small coterie concerned more with satisfying their personal design sense than with achieving a humanist, functional, architecture.[6]

Another leading example of the New Brutalism is the multi-storey housing block built in the Park Hill redevelopment area in Sheffield, designed between 1953 and 1955 by associates of the Smithsons under the supervision of city architect J. L. Womersley, and built between 1957 and 1961 by Ove Arup. Brutalist or not, this complex (not, of course, a tower block) worked well and inspired the loyalty of most of its occupants. One can, in the fifties, detect hints of future discontents, but on the whole the architecture of reconstruction lived up to its claims: the cardinal errors were to be committed during the frantic, and sometimes corrupt, 'redevelopment' of the sixties.

Notes

1 Charles Jencks, *Modern Movements in Architecture* (1973), p. 239.
2 Anthony Jackson, *The Politics of Architecture: A History of Modern Architecture in Britain* (1970), pp. 167–76.
3 Reyner Banham, *The New Brutalism: Ethic or Aesthetic?* (1966), p. 11; Jencks, *Modern Movements*, p. 245.
4 Quoted in Mary Banham and Bevis Hillier (eds), *A Tonic to the Nation: The Festival of Britain 1951* (1976), p. 196.
5 Fiona MacCarthy, *A History of British Design* (1979), pp. 94–5.
6 Jackson, *Politics of Architecture*, p. 183. In general, see the section by Paul Thompson in Peter Kidson, Peter Murray and Paul Thompson (eds), *A History of English Architecture* (1979).

6 The Mass Media

The undoubted economic fact that Hollywood dominated the production and distribution of films in Britain has led to a number of generalizations, based more on assertion than detailed evidence, in particular (a) that there was a widespread Americanization of British life, and (b) that the British people vastly preferred American films to their native products. Most recently, some of these views have been presented in Paul Swann's *The Hollywood Feature Film in Post-War Britain* (1987), though in fact Swann himself recognizes that Sydney Bernstein's Granada chain survey of 1946 'evidenced surprising support for British films'[1]. The Americanization thesis, too, has to be approached with great caution: it originates from a neo-Marxist analysis which attributes the failure of Marxist predictions to come true to the unexpected rise of the American way of life. Much of what is described as Americanization is in fact really modernization (though it would be difficult to disagree that the popular music of the time was American-dominated, Ted Heath being but a poor response to the American Swing bands, as Vera Lynn − 'wartime forces' sweetheart' − and Donald Pears were to crooners and ballad singers Bing Crosby, Guy Mitchell and Doris Day). Undoubtedly British audiences enjoyed the high technical standards of American cinema and, also, the elements of fantasy. Undoubtedly, too, there was a special and peculiar appeal inherent in the great international Hollywood stars, women looking to the female stars for hints on dress, deportment and fashion, men to the male stars as role models.

Cinema attendances reached a peak in 1946, and continued

to be high for a further decade. Central Office of Information Enquiries conducted in March and October 1946 revealed that 32 per cent of the adult civilian population went to the cinema at least once a week, that 13 per cent went more than once, and only 24 per cent did not go at all. Among children of school age 65 per cent went to the cinema at least once a week or more, and only 5 per cent did not go at all. On balance women were more frequent attenders than men, and, as was to be expected, young people went more often than old people. While the cinema attracted its audience from all economic groups, the higher-paid sections of the working class went more frequently than others. Relatively high proportions of factory workers and of clerical and distributive workers (about 40 per cent) went to the cinema once a week or more, whereas a high proportion of professional and managerial workers went less frequently, and about half of retired or unoccupied persons did not go at all. Housewives, the survey reported, went with 'average frequency'. Working-class children were more frequent attenders than middle- and upper-class children.[2] What these audiences saw, to repeat, were largely American films, mainly musicals and romances; there were serious films of social realism, produced in particular by Warner Brothers, but the issues, race, gangsterism, civic corruption, were all rather remote from British experience.

Now let me turn to the domestic product.[3] The quota system, introduced in 1927 and strengthened by the Labour government, was intended to ensure that 30 per cent of feature films were British. Some British film makers tried to operate this legislation to the enrichment of British cinema; others simply produced shoddy 'quota quickies' to fill up the quotas as speedily as possible. Among the most contemptuous critics of British film-making have been British intellectuals themselves, their criticism being two-pronged: first, British films are said not to exploit the potentialities of the medium as an art form, being in formal terms highly conventional and wedded to naturalism; second, they are attacked for reinforcing the dominant values of British society, failing to present that alternative ideology and critique of society which, according to Marxist cultural theory, is the function of good art. How big a handicap absence of formal and stylistic innovation is, is a matter of personal taste. As to the second criticism, art has many, many other functions than that of social criticism: if certain films illuminated the way the British actually were, that is no feeble achievement. It is true that the British film industry was an interlinked and overlapping network of production companies, distribution companies and chains of exhibitors, overwhelmingly dominated by one British figure, J. Arthur Rank, and otherwise by the various American companies. Most films were actually *made* by small production companies, but even if the difficult task of raising the production finance was surmounted, the problem of securing distribution was, in a highly monopolistic environment, a potentially crippling one. Two government-sponsored sources of funding proved to be of only minor assistance to independent producers: the 'Eady Levy' on cinema receipts (voluntary in 1950, compulsory after 1957) tended in practice to be distributed more to the rich than to the poor, funding from the National Film Finance Corporation (established 1949) was in the form of loans not grants.[4].

Putting aside the quota quickies, the banal comedies and the B movies (usually stilted crime stories) specifically designed to accompany an American main attraction the more important British films can be grouped under five heads: films of the great classics of English literature, meaning, in effect, Shakespeare and Dickens; films derived from successful West End plays, sometimes containing some elements of social comment; the romantic dramas produced by Gainsborough Films, very popular at the time, and now enjoying some critical favour because of the strong female parts taken by Margaret Lockwood; the films of Ealing Studios, the production company which had come to prominence during the war for its carefully delineated, and gently understated, celebrations of patriotic Britishness; the handful of ambitious and challenging films whose character was determined (as *auteur* theory maintains films should be determined) by the special genius of the director — I am thinking here particularly of Carol Reed and of the Powell and Pressburger team. In addition, a large number of films of variable quality testified to the nation's continuing obsession with its achievements in the Second World War.

One of the greatest, perhaps the greatest, of British wartime films was set in a former age and had, not Germany, but France as the enemy against which patriotic leadership and popular valour were pitted. This, of course, was Laurence Olivier's *Henry V* which, with daring effect, opens in a set representing Shakespeare's Globe Theatre before steadily widening out to some lavishly elaborate naturalistic scenes. Olivier's *Hamlet* (1948), shot in black and white, was in contrast introspective and restrained. The next great spectacular did not come till 1955 when, electric from its opening 'Now is the winter of our discontent . . .', and dynamic in its portrayal of passionate, energetic evil, Olivier's *Richard III* won acclamation as the best British film of the year. The much-respected director David Lean showed himself a master of creating a menacing Dickensian atmosphere of time and place in his *Great Expectations* (1947) and *Oliver Twist* (1948).

It is a legitimate criticism of British cinema that it has depended too heavily on the theatre for its sources, tending then to make not very imaginative equivalents of the well-made play, without exploiting the separate potential of cinema. The plays of Terence Rattigan were almost automatically converted into films. Some additional interest attaches to *The Chiltern Hundreds* (based on a play by William Douglas Home, member of an aristocratic Scottish family) and *The Guinea Pig* (Boulting Brothers, 1948) based on the play by William Chetham Strode who belonged to the same top public school élite. Like so many artefacts of the West End theatre, *The Chiltern Hundreds*, film as well as play, was set, as the critic Kenneth Tynan later put it, among the aristocracy of 'Loamshire'. One has the feeling that in this milieu a Labour government is a nuisance to be coped with, rather than a force which threatens change: in this conventional, but not altogether unrevealing, comedy of 'political consensus' Douglas Home may have been giving away more than he knew. There is a still more precise political reference in *The Guinea Pig*: the proposal put forward by the wartime Fleming Report, and endorsed by the incoming Labour government, that while the public schools should not be abolished, they should take a higher proportion of boys from less advantaged backgrounds. 'The guinea pig' of the title is the son of a tobacconist in a working-class area (Walthamstow in East London), who as an experiment in advance of any legislation, becomes a pupil at Saintbury school, modelled on Sherborne, though with, in the film, exterior shots taken at Haleybury and Mill Hill. The mood and meaning, very appropriate to much of what was happening at the time, is that of moderate, well-intentioned, upper-class-led reform. It is remarkable how frequently and consistently institutions of educational privilege appear in popular culture (in such comics as *Hotspur* and *Rover*, for instance) as well as élite. A very popular American film at the end of the war was *A Yank at Oxford*; Rattigan's public-school-based *The Browning Version* was made into a successful film in 1951.

The Gainsborough films were set in an English past and reflected the idioms of the eighteenth-century English social novel, the best example being *The Wicked Lady* (1945), directed by Leslie Arliss and featuring two of the three top British box-office attractions of the time, James Mason and Margaret Lockwood (the third was Stewart Granger). But it was the Ealing films which established an image of Britishness, *both* genuinely related to existing characteristics and quirks of British manners and morals, particularly within the spectrum between upper and upper middle class (the 'educated' classes) on one side, and lower middle and upper working class (the 'popular' classes) on the other, *and* tending to set in aspic manners and modes that were fast disappearing in the 'real' post-war world. Though the general tone is moderately reformist, poking fun at grouse-moor aristocrats and the pomposities of power, criticism as often as not is of the bureaucracy, rationing and restrictions associated with the Labour government.

The classic Ealing comedy of post-war society is *Passport to Pimlico* (directed by South African-born Henry Cornelius); the most wickedly stylish and witty, *Kind Hearts and Coronets* (directed by Cambridge graduate Robert Hamer, 1949), which is set in the late nineteenth century. The former is very much a period piece, in which an eccentric aristocratic lady discovers that Pimlico (an inner London suburb as yet ungentrified) belongs to Burgundy, giving the locals the opportunity to set up an independent populist commonwealth, the enemies being the bumbling civil servants played by Basil Radford and Naunton Wayne. Two years earlier Hamer had directed *It Always Rains on Sunday* (starring Googie Withers), which genuinely does create some of the structures and ambience of working-class life in East London and which, in dealing with the tracking down of a violent escaped prisoner, manages to make some critical comments on judicial corporal punishment (finally abolished by the Labour government in 1948). *Whisky Galore* (1949), directed by Boston born, Glasgow educated Alexander Mackendrick, is another tale of local people defying bureaucracy. Ealing attempted a serious police drama in *The Blue Lamp* (1950), the first to feature a new folk hero, P. C. George Dixon (he was actually killed in the film, but that did not stop him being revived for innumerable future television series). *His Excellency* (Robert Hamer, 1952) concerned the eventual establishment of a *modus vivendi* between a new working-class, Labour-appointed, governor general (played by Eric Portman) of a colonial naval base (Malta?) and his upper-class second-in-command (played by Cecil Parkinson); the ostensible message of political consensus is less striking than the blatant racism. With *The Lavender Hill Mob* (Charles Crighton, 1951) Ealing turned more and more to openly criminal activities as the basis for their comedies; this direction continued with *The Ladykillers* (Alexander Mackendrick, 1955). The best days of Ealing were over.

Powell and Pressburger had produced two great wartime fables, *The Life and Death of Colonel Blimp* and *A Canterbury Tale*, the former about a decent old codger somewhat at odds with the morality of modern total war, the latter evoking a Britain which will reassert its best traditions in a better post-war world. *The Red Shoes* (1948) was almost unique in British film-making in being related to a classical art form, ballet (which was, though, as we have noted, expanding in popularity at this time), with references to the composing of a contemporary opera. It interweaves the fable of the ballet, the red shoes which take over from the ballerina and will not stop dancing, with a contemporary story concerning the relentless and almost inhuman dedication of the ballet company's director (Anton Walbrook), and the conflicts of love and artistic dedication between the ballerina (a matchless performance by Moira Shearer) and her husband (Marius Goring), the composer of a successful opera. This film ranks alongside Carol Reed's masterpiece *The Third Man* (1949). In 1946 Reed had demonstrated his gift, through expressionistic use of the camera, for creating menacing mood and atmosphere in *Odd Man Out*, which follows the different loaded encounters of a wounded IRA gunman on the run (James Mason); this was followed by *The Fallen Idol* (1948), equally intense, though more restricted in range. The original notion of creating a thriller out of the idea of a missing third man, vital witness to a motor accident, and the original screenplay, came from Graham Greene. However, comparison of that screenplay with the film as finally released shows how the production was in fact dominated by Reed, with interventions (it is to Reed's credit that he welcome these) from the great American actor and director who played the 'third man', Orson Welles. Set in war-shattered Vienna, *The Third Man* is *the* film of post-war Europe, divided between Russia and the West. The main protagonists are a naive American writer of popular westerns (Joseph Cotten) and a commonsense British officer (Trevor Howard); both, for different reasons, seek the haunting figure of Harry Lime (the zither theme by Anton Karas is brilliantly used), who turns out to be utterly evil. The film is about friendship, loss of naivety, different kinds of love, the status of art, the balance between evil enforced by circumstance and inherent evil; the sudden shafts of wit are side-splitting; the last sequence in which the girl with whom the novelist has fallen in love (Alida Valli), but who remains faithful to the memory of Harry Lime for all his evil, simply walks unheedingly past him, is brilliantly effective. Direct government intervention in the film industry achieved real artistic success when the state-sponsored company Group Three produced *The Brave Don't Cry* (1952), which, most unusually, created, with great sensitivity, an industrial working-class community, a Scottish mining village, under the impact of a tragic mining disaster, modelled loosely on the actual Knockshinnoch disaster.

An innovation of the fifties was the X certificate: but the handful issued went either to manifestly exploitation films, or to minority problem films; the bulk went to imported French films, it being conventionally accepted that French films could deal with the kinds of topic, and present the kinds of character which were alien to the gentle traditions of British cinema. On the whole, the wartime revival appeared to be over. When *Lucky Jim* was put on the screen by the Boulting brothers in 1957 it was in an utterly debased form which simply turned the book into a pointless farce. However, there was one other film of outstanding merit, David Lean's *Bridge on the River Kwai* (1957), an epic of the war in Burma where a stubborn, cantankerous, British officer (played by Alec Guinness), forced by the Japanese to build a bridge, becomes fanatically committed to the project when, of course, it was in the interest of the allies that it should be blown up.

Newspapers, at least in their proper role as purveyors of news, fall outside this study. Radio and television,[5] however, have large entertainment elements. At the end of the war the radio services monopolized by the BBC were reorganized into three: the Light Programme, the Home Service Programme, and the Third Programme. The audience research which the BBC had pioneered shortly before the war treated the audiences for these three services as synonymous with working-class, middle-class and upper-middle and upper-class, respectively. The most successful radio soap opera of all time was 'Mrs Dale's Diary', set in a distinctly upper-middle-class milieu. There was a strong feeling within the BBC, dating back to the early years of the war, that working-class voices should also be heard on the air and that something equivalent to a working-class Mrs Dale's Diary ought to be put out. Little success attended these efforts and the working-class Mrs Dale's Diary was never discovered. The Third Programme played an important part in the musical renaissance after 1945; but much of its output was characterized by a mannered pedantry and a distinctive academic parochialism. The most significant phenomenon was the success of 'Saturday Night Theatre' on the Home Service, with an audience at the end of the forties equivalent to one-third of the entire adult population. Here was the precursor of the hegemony of television soon to come: drama and entertainment at the touch of a switch.

Television broadcasting, only just beginning at the end of

the thirties, had been brought to an end by the war; it grew again only slowly in the post-war years though by the early fifties there were 5 million television viewers. In order that television might not become an addiction nor distract children from their studies nor adults from their duties, television broadcasting was confined to a limited number of hours per day – also very much in keeping with the BBC ethic. The first debate over the BBC's position took place in 1954 when, against the convictions of senior Conservatives, the Act was passed which led to the setting up of a separate commercial television channel.

Notes

1 Paul Swann, *The Hollywood Feature Film in Post-War Britain* (1987), p. 39.
2 COI, *The Cinema and the Public* (1946).
3 For British cinema, see Roy Armes, *A Critical History of British Cinema* (1978); and J. Richards and A. Aldgate, *The Best of British* (1986).
4 British Film Institute, *British Film Industry*, typescript compiled by Linda Wood (1980).
5 The standard work is Asa Briggs, *History of Broadcasting in Great Britain*, vol. 4, *Sound and Vision* (1974).

Part II

Great Expectations: 1958–1976

7 New Departures

Changes in lifestyles, living standards, opportunities and patterns of cultural behaviour are apparent in all the Western societies between the late 1950s and late 1960s. A major feature, indeed, is a greater cultural interchange than ever before, along with a marked reversal of the one-way movement from America: Italian espresso machines and Italian fashion; French discos; British pubs, British pop music, and British pop design; European film directors and a medley of European film actors and actresses. Many of the developments to be discussed in this chapter, then, are international; some, in origins at least, are specifically British.

The phrase 'cultural revolution', which I have used on a number of occasions,[1] may or may not be an apt one. It is certainly contentious. From the left it is contended that no fundamental shifts in the structure of power, no serious attacks on the deprivations suffered by substantial minorities, took place, and that those features of sixties culture which hit the headlines were shallow, commercial and sexist. From the right, it is argued that the steady abandonment since the war of older disciplines and older values escalated into an orgy of self-indulgence supported on income which had not been earned. Mrs Thatcher's comment of March 1982 is well known: 'We are reaping what was sown in the Sixties ... fashionable theories and permissive claptrap set the scene for a society in which the old virtues of discipline and restraint were denigrated.'[2] Certainly, what happened between the late fifties and the early seventies was not a political revolution, not a revolution in economic thought and practice; but it was, I believe, a transformation in the opportunities and freedoms available both to the majority as a whole and to distinctive individuals and groups within that majority. These transformations were not imposed from above, nor were they the achievement of a coherent group of 'revolutionaries'. They helped to make possible the events of 1968, but their significance had nothing to do with the success or failure of these events, on which too much attention has been lavished. More critically, the real changes in ordinary lives have been obscured by the attention lavished on the minority practices of 'underground culture' whose long-term influence was minimal.

Fundamental was the marked economic recovery of Western Europe from the early to mid-fifties, creating new kinds of consumer demand both internal, and as already been suggested, international. The principal new markets can be defined as youth, the working class, the provinces, racial minorities and, in lesser degree, women. The new consumers were in a position to reject the canons laid down by established authority, metropolitan, upper-class and old. America was escaping from the insular parochialism which had gripped it during the Cold War period: even in the Mid West outlets appeared for foreign cultural products, including British ones. Hollywood had ossified, so had Tin Pan Alley: therein lay the opportunity. But the challenges to established authority were particularly striking in Britain, partly because Britain had long been such a conservative and homogeneous society, but partly also because Britain had generally been such a sensible society, characterized, as I have expressed it elsewhere, by 'Secular Anglicanism'.[3] The codes of behaviour which had grown up, generally enforced with discretion, were not absurd given their historical context (the economic dependence of women on men, for instance, and of youth on age). Now a country which lacked the antediluvian bigotries of the American Bible Belt, the clerical and anti-clerical factionalism of France and Italy, or the reviving bourgeois stolidity of Christian Democratic Germany, showed itself specially responsive to the new pressures.

British developments can be summed up under six overlapping headings. The first is defined by the two clichés '*affluence*' and *consumerism'*. Average weekly earnings for industrial workers rose 34 per cent between 1955 and 1960 and 130 per cent between 1955 and 1969; average earnings of middle-class salaried employees rose 127 per cent between 1955 and 1969. While prices of food and other necessities were steadily rising (retail prices rose by 63 per cent between 1955 and 1969), the prices of small cars, in relation to earning power, were falling, and many products of new technology such as television sets and washing machines were, despite inflation, actually costing less. Still a rarity in the early 1950s, TV sets were to be found in 75 per cent of homes by 1961, and 91 per cent of homes by 1971.

Second, though the basic *class* structure remained unaltered, there were significant changes in detail and attitudes. The working class became visible and assertive as it had never been before. Some of its most talented escapees held the limelight and while doing so retained, with bravado, working-class accent and manner. The vogue for 'classlessness' was somewhat spurious, but the very advocacy of the notion altered the old indicators of status: 'posh cockney' replaced the plummy Oxford accent. Third, there was the power of, and preoccupation with, *youth*. Both rock-based pop music and pop fashion were products of, and even when fully commercialized remained products for, youth. Fourth, is the transformation in *sexual attitudes* and *behaviour*. The survey material is copious: perhaps the single most significant statistic is that, while in 1951 only 51 per cent of women interviewed had declared sex to be very important in marriage, in 1969 the percentage was 67.[4]

'Permissiveness' was the word brought into use to describe the whole complex of developments within the sexual arena. Yet in characterizing the social legislation of the period a better heading might be that of *fairness towards*, and *freedom for*, each individual. To the fifth heading, I would add a sixth, pervading all aspects of private and communal life, *frankness* and *openness* to the extent of (another word of the time) *'explicitness'*, these together being part of the general reaction against the emollient fibbing of the older generation (including the fashionable clothing, male and female, that concealed the imperfections of form and figure).

In the voting preferences of the British people there were, as ever, no great swings. At the beginning of the sixties the Conservatives were in power, led by the one-nation, patrician Tory, Harold Macmillan. In 1964 Labour scraped into office under Harold Wilson, also very much a consensus politician, going on to win a substantial majority in 1966. In 1970, to the surprise of many, the Conservatives, led by Edward Heath, certainly no fanatic of the radical right, returned to office. Unsuccessful confrontation with the miners pushed Heath into another election early in 1974. Although the Conservatives polled 37.9 per cent of the popular vote, Labour with 37.1 per cent had four more seats and formed a minority government till October when Labour polled 39.2 per cent to 35.9 for the Conservatives. The government of first Wilson, then James Callaghan (yet another middle-of-the-road figure), in effect depended on the support of the Liberals. Continuity is clearly seen in arts policy, as Arts Council funding and local authority initiatives increased. Indeed the entire period could be characterized as marking a culmination of the idea enunciated towards the end of the war of culture as a form of social welfare. The major stages were the transference in 1964 of the source of Arts Council funding from the Treasury to the Department of Education, the appointment of Jennie Lee as Minister for the Arts, and the publication in 1965 of Jennie Lee's government paper *A Policy for the Arts*. In education, too, the sixties marked a climax in post-war developments, with the expansion in higher education providing part of the basis for enhanced interest in artistic and intellectual practices – from opera to feminism.

Outside of consensus politics there were, indeed, mighty political issues, principally hostility to American military policy in general and, above all, to American activities in Viet Nam in particular, revulsion against the commercialism of contemporary society and the power of multi-national corporations, and protests over nuclear weaponry. These matters of concern often appeared in 'alternative' or 'underground' culture. Yet that very culture also benefited from Arts Council and local authority patronage.

The key Acts of the period were not part of some political blueprint for transforming society, but resulted from pressures generated from within society: 1960, the Betting and Gaming Act (recognizing working-class vices as well as more aristocratic ones); 1967, the Abortion Act, the National Health Service (the Family Planning) Act and the Sexual Offences Act (legalizing homosexual acts between two consenting adults in private); 1968, the Theatres Act (abolishing censorship); 1969 the Representation of the People Act (reducing the voting age to eighteen) and the Divorce Reform Act; 1970 the Matrimonial Property Act (establishing that a wife's work, whether as a housewife within the home or as a money-earner outside it, should be considered as an equal contribution towards creating the family home if, as a result of divorce, that had to be divided), the Equal Pay Act (imperfect, certainly, and not intended to become fully effective for another five years) and the Chronic Sick and Disabled Persons Act (which symbolized and ratified the new openness towards the problems of the disabled). Acts of Parliament must never be mistaken for the reality of social change; but in fact the reality of change was palpable in the archaeology of everyday life, in attitudes, behaviour and artefacts. Of course, there were many sources of tension and deprivation—race relations and high-rise housing for instance. This era was not a golden age, simply a time of release and change.

Mrs Thatcher, indeed, was right, if for the phrase 'the old virtues of discipline and restraint were denigrated' we substitute 'the social controls established by the Victorians were overthrown'. This was a revolution which could not easily be reversed since, in fact, it had little to do with the state and everything to do with society. It was not a revolution towards socialism, but if it had its too-evident male chauvinist aspects it also contributed to the launching, partly in response to the manifestations of decontrolled male sexuality, of activist feminism. The culture of the day was influenced by these developments, contributed greatly to them, and indeed was an integral part of Britain's striking new departures.

Notes

1 See my *Class: Image and Reality in Britain, France and the USA since 1930* (1980, new edn 1990), ch. 14; *British Society since 1945* (1982, new edn 1990); '*Room at the Top, Saturday Night and Sunday Morning* and the Cultural Revolution in Britain', in *Journal of Contemporary History*, vol. 19 (1984), pp. 127–52; and 'The 1960s: was there a "Cultural Revolution"?', in *Contemporary Record*, vol. 2, no. 3, Autumn 1988.

2 Quoted by Brian Masters, *The Swinging Sixties* (1985), p. 5.

3 See my *Social Change in the Twentieth Century* (1970), and *British Society since 1945*, pp. 16, 154, 155, 264, 275.

4 Geoffrey Gorer, *Sex and Marriage in England Today* (1970), p. 91.

8 'The Snobbery that Used to Exist ...'

The central role of cinema

Rick Wakeman was one of a number of musicians who moved from a strictly classical training into the world of pop music. He explained to Michael Cable, chronicler of the pop industry, that:

the whole attitude to serious pop music is changing in the colleges and academies ... Even members of the staff, the tutors and the professors, are beginning to accept that at the top end of the scale rock is musically valued. The snobbery that used to exist is gradually disappearing ...[1]

How far, and in what ways, were barriers between different 'levels' of culture flattened?

Here I want to begin by looking at the conversion of Braine's novel *Room at the Top* into a popular film carried out by Romulus Films (a company with a profitable specialization in 'problem' films for minority audiences). Romulus employed three competent professionals, Jack Clayton to direct, Neil Paterson to write the screenplay, and Mario Nascimbene to produce the musical score, and one very distinguished one, cameraman Freddie Francis. As was the custom, the film was planned throughout it consultation with the British Board of Film Censors. What becomes utterly clear from the censorship correspondence[2] is that, influenced by wider trends in British society, the censorship was itself changing its views as to what was now acceptable to British audiences. Where it did put up a fight (usually over words like 'bitch' and 'lust'), it nearly always gave way in the end. By concentrating, altering and frequently developing material in the novel, the film presents two major preoccupations (or 'meanings'): class power, class rigidities and the possibility of social mobility; and sex, frankly presented and still more frankly discussed. As visual medium, the film gives very strong representations of the physical differences in social environments. While Joe Lampton in the novel was fastidious and self-questioning, Joe Lampton in the film is straightforwardly predatory, a figure much more likely to impact strongly on mass audiences. Almost every sequence of the film makes a clear statement about class or about sex, and sometimes both; no such commentary could be applied to the chapters of the novel.

Two other strikingly original films were released in 1959. Film director Basil Dearden had, it is true, dealt with the problem of racial prejudice in *Pool of London* (1950), honourably but rather flabbily: his *Sapphire* was unique in bringing to the screen a whole varied community of blacks – the film was very directly a response to the Notting Hill race riots of August 1958. Unlike *Room at the Top*, and the vast majority of British films of the time, *Sapphire* was shot in colour: in an article in *Kine Weekly* in December 1958, Dearden explained that his idea was to throw the sombre London background 'into contrast with the sudden splashes of colour introduced by the coloured people themselves'.[3]

I'm All Right Jack (Boulting Bros) features some of the same characters as the 1956 *Private's Progress*, but is in all respects a different order of film. That it was a highly deliberate and historically sensitive social satire is made clear by the very self-conscious pre-credit sequence, sketching the history of the decline of the old upper class since 1945, when it had been rooted in the world of finance, to the present, when its representatives are, somewhat shadily, involved in industry. Ian Carmichael plays Stanley, an earnest and gormless young man, who has been 'brought up a gentleman'. At his university appointments board he is told that what is required above all is 'an air of confidence'. The atmosphere on the factory floor, the working-class accents and attitudes, are beautifully established, with only the necessary minimum of satirical exaggeration. Plenty of previous British films had presented the distinctions of class, but till *I'm All Right Jack* class was represented as something which held the country together: now it was being shown as something highly destructive.

Room at the Top had reversed a standard process in taking a literary artefact and making it stronger and more shocking. Normalcy was restored in Tony Richardson's production of *Look Back in Anger.* 'How long does it take a sensational, shocking, and timely play to become easily digestible and mildly dated?' critic Leonard Mosley shrewdly asked in the *Daily Express.* 'Answer: the time it takes to transfer it from the stage to the screen.'[4] And the capacity of the industry to turn out the same old rubbish had not yet noticeably diminished. Within months of *I'm All Right Jack*, the Boulting Brothers were offering the pathetic farce *The French Mistress*; political acuity of any sort was utterly lacking in the vacuous 'political comedy', *Left, Right and Centre*, once again with Ian Carmichael, produced and directed by Launder and Gilliat.

However, as we move into the sixties, it becomes clear that British cinema was taking up a new central role, not just living off, but developing and bringing together new sources of talent. Early successes brought prestige; prestige brought American investment. But the new sources of talent were entirely native: novelists, playwrights and actors with provincial and/or working-class backgrounds, beneficiaries of new educational opportunities and, sometimes, of the expansion of provincial theatre. Three influences percolated through the written and spoken word and into film: provincial realism, social criticism, often explicitly socialist, and the non-naturalistic psychological exploration of the dynamics of personal relationships. Among the 'provincial realists' one can number Alan Sillitoe (b. Nottingham, 1928), Willis Hall and Keith Waterhouse (both b. Leeds, 1929), Stan Barstow (b. 1928) and David Storey (b. 1933), both sons of Yorkshire miners and educated at grammar school, and Shelagh Delaney (b. Salford, 1939). The leading socialist dramatist was Arnold Wesker (b. 1932 in the East End of London), whose first success, *Chicken Soup with Barley* (1958), was presented at the Belgrade Theatre, Coventry, which was also responsible for first productions of *Roots* (1959) and *I'm Talking About Jerusalem* (1960), these three plays forming a trilogy involving an East London left-wing Jewish family and farm labourers in Norfolk over a period of 30 years. Most original, and in some ways most influential, was Harold Pinter (b. 1920), son of an East London Jewish tailor, who, after grammar school, became a professional actor. Pinter, manifestly influenced by Beckett, used the banal, everyday repetitions of language to explore the ways in which power relationships between human beings can shift, often quite frighteningly. His first play, *The Room*, was presented in 1957. Old-guard metropolitan critics nearly killed *The Birthday Party* (1958), but Pinter's distinctive voice quickly gained recognition among theatre audiences around the country, and in the quality and popular press. There followed *The Caretaker* (1960), *The Lover* (1963), *The Homecoming* (1965), *Old Times* (1971), *No Man's Land* (1975) and *Betrayal* (1978).

The most successful films of the early sixties fall into the category of social realism (though many explored very particular areas of personal experience). There then developed something of a preoccupation with change in contemporary Britain: the permissive society, the pop scene, 'Singing London'. Yet at the same time British cinema developed two types of highly distinctive fantasy, the Bond movies and the Hammer horror films. Finally, completely new areas of experience were explored, or new kinds of social criticism were developed, often in non-naturalistic ways.

Alan Sillitoe was born into the highly deprived family of a tannery labourer. He left school in 1942 and went to work first in the Raleigh bicycle factory in Nottingham, then with a plywood manufacturer, and subsequently with an engineering firm. As had been the case with John Braine, the war had a considerable effect on the development of his career. Sillitoe became a cadet in the Air Training Corps, seizing the unique opportunity to study new skills. As soon as he was old enough, he joined the RAF and, in the immediate post-war years, was sent out as a radio operator to Malaya. There is another strange link with Braine in that while in Malaya he contracted

TB. He was in hospital for a year in 1948, and tried his hand at various pieces of writing. Sillitoe, now, was certainly no typical representative of the working class: with his RAF pension he deliberately established himself as a writer, working briefly in Nottingham, then in south east France, and finally in Majorca. The theme of the irresponsible hedonism of Saturday night and the slow, ineluctable patterns of life, represented by Sunday morning, had fascinated him for some time. Ten years after its first publication, Sillitoe wrote that 'the greatest inaccuracy was ever to call the book a "working-class novel" for it is really nothing of the sort. It is simply a novel ...'[5] On the other hand, of course, working-class figures were the figures he knew; the working-class milieu was the proper setting for his story — in that sense *Saturday Night and Sunday Morning* was a working-class novel.

Sillitoe's novel appeared in October 1958, just three months before the film of *Room at the Top*. Although reviewers of the latter did not refer to *Saturday Night and Sunday Morning*, it was itself far more radical than Braine's novel and played its part, in the more restricted circles of novel readers, in the growing acceptance of the importance of hitherto neglected geographical and social sections of British society, and also of a particular sexual frankness. The screen rights were bought by Woodfall Films, the new company founded by John Osborne and Tony Richardson, ostensibly to allow the voices of anger, kitchen sink, provinces and working class to be heard, but backed by Canadian producer Harry Saltzman who made no secret of his wish to turn an honest penny or two out of the new fashions.[6] The director was Karel Reisz, who had been a leading figure in the 'New Cinema' documentary movement of the fifties. Sillitoe himself was commissioned to write the screenplay. A poet and a writer, Sillitoe had no affinity with cinema, and the final script, as ever in the world of film, was a team effort, with, of course, the British Board of Film Censors playing their part.

Much of the poetic ambivalence of the novel is lost, and the boy (Arthur Seaton, played by Albert Finney)-meets-girl (Doreen, played by Shirley Anne Field) element greatly strengthened. None the less, the essential, and novel, ambiance of the film is firmly established in an important pre-credit sequence where we see Arthur as his lathe. The censors objected to four things in the original screenplay: 'the slap-happy successful termination of pregnancy'; *'language'*; love scenes 'too revealing'; and the violence of Arthur's beating-up. In the film finally released, the alteration in the abortion episode is the most obvious single change: we are left in no doubt that the attempt with hot water and gin has failed. Bert, only one of many colourful and vicious characters in the novel (educated in remand homes and Borstal), very much cleaned up, becomes Arthur's boon companion. The violence and the villainy are played down, so that essentially we are in the realm of the respectable working class (with which, of course, mass audiences could readily identify): a class point is therefore made much more clearly, the sense of working-class awareness and identity comes through all the more strongly.

The film *The Angry Silence* (1960), based on a story by Michael Craig and Richard Gregson, was not an outstanding commercial success — it could too readily be portrayed as union-bashing — but it was an important film in the way in which it meticulously built up a factory environment and re-produced the resonances of working-class speech. Woodfall's screen adaptation of Osborne's *The Entertainer* (1960) was in-finitely more successful than their adaptation of *Look Back in Anger*, perhaps because the later play had a much wider his-torical significance. *Victim* (1961), directed by Basil Dearden from an original screenplay, was a genuinely daring and honourable film in dealing with homosexuality within a con-temporary setting (two films of 1960, *Oscar Wilde* and *The Trials of Oscar Wilde*, were more safely pushed back in time—all three films should be seen in the context of the Wolfenden Report of 1957 which eventually led to the decriminalizing of adult homosexuality). *The Kitchen* (1961) was adapted from the play of the same name by Arnold Wesker (1959), brilliantly using its setting on the working side of a restaurant to make pointed social comments. *A Taste of Honey* (1961), in which a teenager expecting a mixed race baby, is befriended by a homosexual, was from Shelagh Delaney's play, as *A Kind of Loving* (marking the directorial debut of John Schlesinger) was based on Barstow's novel, the story of an office worker whose high cultural aspirations are destroyed as he finds himself lumbered with a marriage which represents no more than 'a kind of loving'. Alan Sillitoe's novella about a Borstal boy who, despite the governor, refuses to complete a race which he could easily win, *The Loneliness of the Long Distance Runner* (1962), formed the basis for Tony Richardson's Woodfall film of the same name. *This Sporting Life* (1963), about the pain and pride of that very working-class, but, of course, not typical figure, the rugby league footballer, was an outstanding film, directed by left-wing but upper-class Lindsay Anderson, from David Storey's astonishing novel.

Sixties films have quite properly been accused of what later became known as male chauvinism, yet one should not overlook the emancipated young woman played by Julie Christie in *Billy Liar*, her amoral *Darling* (1965) and her spirited Bathsheba in *Far From the Madding Crowd* (1967) from the classic Hardy novel, all directed by John Schlesinger; nor the sophisticated (and lustful) Joan Greenwood in Tony Richardson's rumbustious (and permissive) representation of Fielding's *Tom Jones* (1963 – again featuring Albert Finney). To these should be added full-blooded performances by Rachel Roberts in *Saturday Night and Sunday Morning* and *This Sporting Life*, the leading parts played by Rita Tushingham and Dora Bryan in *A Taste of Honey*, the self-contained Lesley Caron deciding on her own to have her illegitimate child in *The L-Shaped Room* (a 1962 Romulus film directed by Bryan Forbes from the novel by Lynne Reid Banks), and the ruthless Charlotte Rampling happy to abandon her child, the sturdy Lynn Redgrave, ready to adopt it, in *Georgy Girl* (1966).

Alfie (1966, directed by Lewis Gilbert from the play, much recycled, by Bill Naughton) epitomized the cheerfully amoral working-class swinger, played by Michael Caine, and the whole atmosphere of permissiveness. Censorship, however, was by no means dead as was made clear by the fate of *The Party's Over* (1963, directed by Guy Hamilton, and featuring Oliver Reed, nephew of the great director) which, because it did not sufficiently condemn the beatnik lifestyle it portrayed, was held up for two years and subjected to certain alterations. *To Sir with*

Love (1966), the not-very-successful film based on a fifties novel, added to the problem school scenario the advent of a black teacher (played by Sidney Poitier). *Catch Us if you Can* (1965) featured the pop group the Dave Clark Five, and marked the film debut of television director John Boorman, very much a man of the cultural revolution in that he clearly thought of himself as at home on both sides of the Atlantic. It took the American-born Richard Lester to capture the surrealistic humour of top pop group The Beatles in *A Hard Day's Night* (1964) and *Help!* (1965). *Smashing Time* (1967, directed by Desmond Davis) incorporated the clothing revolution of Carnaby Street. Permissive life in the provinces formed the context for Michael Winner's *The System* (1964), known in America as *The Girl Getters*, Swinging London that for *The Jokers* (1966) and *I'll Never Forget What's 'is Name* (1967).

Save for the occasional elements of surrealism, the overwhelming number of such films were naturalistic in presentation. It is part of the Pinter mode to appear naturalistic, save that through the naturalism there penetrate the menaces, the ambitions, the lusts of the subconscious. Clive Donner's film of *The Caretaker* (1963) was very different from anything that had yet appeared on the British screen. Donner's next film, *Nothing but the Best* (1964), was more conventional, a take-off of *Room at the Top* combined with the satire, updated by a decade, of *I'm All Right Jack*: the central character (unlike the Ian Carmichael figure) has not been born into the upper class, but he makes his way there by acquiring the same completely empty, gentlemanly, qualities – he doesn't learn any history, but he learns the upper-class affectation of referring to all historical characters as 'bloody' ('bloody Napoleon') and to leading historians by their first names (*Alan* Taylor, *Hugh* Trevor-Roper). Meantime the American director Joseph Losey, domiciled in Britain as a refugee from McCarthyism, had made *The Servant* (1963), a 'Pinteresque' drama about a gentleman's gentleman gaining the upper hand over his rich gentleman: the screenplay in fact was by Pinter. Early in January 1967 there was released *Accident*, directed by Joseph Losey with a screenplay by Harold Pinter (from the novel by Nicholas Mosley). Brilliantly structured (beginning, and ending with the accident of the title), beautifully scripted, this film with its young aristocrat (Michael Yorke) and Oxford dons (Dirk Bogarde and Stanley Baker), in ambience is many miles from the provincial settings of the films of the beginning of the decade; far more critically, it, even more than they, was a far cry, in its utterly persuasive explorations of the realities and ambiguities of human behaviour, from previous eras of British film-making. Britain, it might be said, was ready for *the* film of the London-centred international revolution of the sixties, *Blow Up*, by the Italian director Antonioni which followed before January was out. Made in England with an entirely British cast, it had behind it the wealth and power of Metro Goldwyn Mayer. According to MGM's press release: 'The story is set against the world of fashion, dolly girls, pop groups, beat clubs, models, parties, and above all, the "in" photographers who more than anyone have promoted the city's new image.'

Photography I shall leave till chapter 10, concentrating here on Thomas, the modish photographer of the film, played by David Hemmings. The strong narrative element of the film is in the form of a kind of thriller: the blow-up of a photograph Thomas has taken seems to reveal a murder; an elegant young lady (Vanessa Redgrave) attempts to retrieve the photograph. One scene which attracted much attention involved Hemmings tumbling around the floor with a troop of scantily clad teeny-boppers. In the final sequence, presumably designed to point up the film's theme of the problematic nature of reality and truth, Thomas watches a mimed tennis match, his eyes mechanically following the invisible ball backwards and forwards; then the noise of the ball being struck comes on to the sound-track, but still no ball can be seen. Within a visually rich series of images operating on many levels, the dialogue itself is very effective: it was largely written by another playwright making his name on the London stage, Edward Bond, of whom more later.

Lindsay Anderson's *If* (1968) (the title carries a deliberate anti-Kipling allusion) starts naturalistically in a public school with three highly individualistic school boys being subjected to repressive and brutal discipline; the film then moves into a violent climax, presumably intended to be of considerable symbolic force, when the Founder's Day celebration is bombed and machine-gunned by the rebel boys. Very much an art film, one could say, without the *cachet* of Antonioni, or the attractions of Swinging London. Production was by Memorial Enterprises, founded by sixties prodigy Albert Finney and headed by the older actor Michael Medwin, who, however, had great difficulty in finding financial backing. Ultimately the American company Paramount provided backing, but even then exhibition was confined to the Paramount cinema in London. There, the film was sufficiently successful commercially for the ABC circuit to agree to national release in 1969. The censors removed shots of male genitalia but permitted the sequence of the not very erotic matron wandering through the dormitories in full frontal nude exposure.[7] Another distinctive talent was that of Ken Russell who, from the documentary style of his TV film about Elgar, moved to the lavish, expressionistic *The Music Lovers* (1970), based (loosely) on the life of Tchaikovsky. Ken Loach's *Kes* (1969), telling the story of an underprivileged boy in the North East and his relationship with a kestrel, was in some ways a reversion to gritty social realism: but it was also highly poetic. *Sunday Bloody Sunday* (1971), based on the triangle of handsome young man lusted after by both a highly intelligent woman (Glenda Jackson) and an elegant homosexual (Peter Finch), was characteristic of the competent and mature work of filmic art that the British industry was now capable of producing. However, it was true that while most of the characteristic films of the sixties had, despite their stylistic traditionalism, achieved considerable reputations abroad, British films of the 1970s were less widely recognized.

One figure who did command international attention was Nicholas Roeg, who had been cameraman on *The Caretaker*, *Nothing but the Best*, Truffaut's *Fahrenheit 451* (his British film of 1966 with Julie Christie) and *Far from the Madding Crowd*. In 1968 Roeg collaborated with painter and writer Donald Cammell, author of the original script for *Performance*, in directing the film with that title. An art film, full of complex allusions, consciously aiming to emulate Bergman and Antonioni, *Performance* faced enormous difficulties in finding producers and distributors, and was not indeed released till late 1970. Backing from the American Warner Brothers was only secured because of the commitment of rock star Mick Jagger to playing the leading role of Turner. In the words of enthusiast Roy Armes, *Performance*:

begins as a violent thriller making explicit links between the capitalist business world and the underworld of protection rackets and intimidation, and following the exploits of the strong-arm man Chas (James Fox), whose taste for needless brutality eventually compels him to go into hiding from both the police and his employers. His chosen hiding place is the Notting Hill home of Turner, a drop-out-ex-pop star now living in an androgynous *ménage à trois*. Under the influence of drugs and the bizarre behaviour of Turner and the two women (Michelle Breton and Anita Pallenberg), Chas loses his certainly of his own identity. He and Turner, outwardly so dissimilar, come to be two halves of a single personality in an atmosphere where dream and reality fuse and even the separation of male and female no longer holds true.[8]

Walkabout (1971), concerning two middle-class Australian children (the elder played by Jenny Agutter) adrift in the Australian desert and befriended by an Aborigine, operates both as a children's adventure yarn and as a more complex cultural study, ending with the suicide of the Aborigine as he feels himself rebuffed by the elder child. Some of the nudity is breathtaking.

There could be no account of British film-making in this period without reference to the James Bond films and the famous horror films produced by Hammer. With regard to these, and certain other films, which could not unreasonably be defined as escapist and, indeed, in large measure exploitative, three points can be made. First, one area in which the British film industry did indisputably lead the world was that of special effects; these films called upon that superiority to a spectacular degree. Second, there were, in most of the films here being considered, elements of humorous self-mockery. Third, and largely consequent upon these two other points, the British fantasy films of the time can definitely lay claim to a certain stylishness.

Ian Fleming's novels about secret agent 007 James Bond were extremely popular towards the end of the fifties (and for the next thirty odd years). They are full of sex (or implied sex), violence and a snobbish knowingness about the luxuries of life. In 1961, Harry Saltzman combined with the American producer Albert 'Cubby' Broccoli in buying the options on all the Bond novels except *Casino Royale*, which Fleming had already sold, and set up a six-picture contract with United Artists. Three suave screen heroes were considered for the part of James Bond, Patrick McGoohan, Richard Johnson and Roger Moore. But Broccoli had taken a liking to Sean Connery in, of all things, the 1959 Disney film *Darby O'Gill and the Little People*. Fleming's reaction to Connery was that he 'was looking for Commander James Bond, not an overgrown stunt man'. Connery spoke with a marked Edinburgh accent, one which, however, is slow and easy to follow, and suggests a kind of mid-Atlantic quality. Film director Terence Young undertook to induct Connery into the patrician sensibilities of Commander Bond; it was Connery himself who decided to play the role tongue-in-cheek and who wrote in some of the ironic one-liners which became the distinguishing feature of the role.[9] But what got the biggest laughs from the largest cinema audiences in this period was the series of very traditionally British vulgar comedies, the 'Carry On' films: from *Carry On Sergeant* (1958) to *Carry On Emmanuelle* (1978) there were twenty-seven.

Discussing the most distinctive of British films is not the same as describing what British audiences saw. The most popular of all sixties films (one Welsh woman went to see it every day for a year)[10] was *The Sound of Music*, whose schmaltzy sentimentality is well summed up in the alternative title 'The Sound of Mucus'. Steadily, however, Hollywood was exporting innovative films which tended to reinforce the trends already being established by British films. *Lolita* was striking not only for its permissiveness but also because effectively its star was Englishman Peter Sellers, who was encouraged by director Stanley Kubrick to exploit his improvisational talents; it was also filmed in London. Kubrick's *Doctor Strangelove or: How I learned to stop worrying and love the bomb* (1964) again featured Sellers, and to accommodate him was shot at Shepperton

Studios near London. Kubrick's *2001: A Space Oddessy*, and especially its psychedelic trip sequence, acquired a cult appeal particularly for youth and the 'underground' (see chapter 10). Other films to which the perhaps slightly questionable term 'cult' film can be applied, but which were certainly also widely popular, were *Hud* (1963) with Paul Newman as a cowboy anti-hero, *The Graduate* (1967), with Dustin Hoffman as the student with whom at least some of Britain's expanding university population could identify, and with music by Simon and Garfunkel, and *Bonnie and Clyde*, using nostalgia to glamourize violent crime. (A much gentler, but more profoundly satirical, version was *Butch Cassidy and the Sundance Kid* of 1969, featuring two of Hollywood's handsomest men, Paul Newman and Robert Redford.) The first spaghetti western, Sergio Leone's *Fistful of Dollars*, featuring Clint Eastwood, arrived here in 1967. Violence reached higher levels and more explicit presen-tation than ever before in Sam Peckinpah's *The Wild Bunch* (1968). *Easy Rider* (1969) introduced two motor-cycle riding hippies, Peter Fonda and Dennis Hopper, the film being marked (some said marred) by a good deal of ad-libbing. British direc-tor John Schlesinger was responsible for *Midnight Cowboy* (1969), with Jon Voight as the would-be Texan stud who fails to take New York women by storm and ends up in a touch-ing relationship with the deformed Ratso, played by Dustin Hoffman.

The successes of British films in the sixties, whose actual production had largely been carried out by small independent companies operating in a variety of studios, had been sustained by American investment: the Union Jack was a highly bankable label. In the early seventies, in parallel with international trends, the industry went into sharp recession: the American trans-national EMI took over much of the British capacity, and many studios were closed down. Still, some distinguished, or at least distinctive, films were made: two satires on contemporary life (on soap operas and slick salesmanship, respectively), *The National Health*, directed by Jack Gold from the play by Peter Nichols, with music by Carl Davis, and *O lucky man*, directed by Lindsay Anderson from the original story by Malcolm McDowell who played the role of Mick Travis, in 1973; two further stages in the controversial career of Ken Russell, *Mahler* (1974) and *Lisztomania* (1975); and the first transposition to the large screen of the eccentric television series which had a cult following in the United States, *Monty Python and the Holy Grail* (1975). Continuing preeminence in special effects was demonstrated in *Live and Let Die* (1973), the first Bond movie to feature Roger Moore in place of Sean Connery who aspired to more serious roles, and *The Golden Voyage of Sinbad*, also 1973. But the manner in which the liberating permissiveness of the sixties had deteriorated into commercialized crud is well represented by titles of late 1974 and early 1975 respectively, *Can you keep it up for a week?*, and *Eskimo Nell* (the title being derived from the classic bawdy song).

The rise of television

In the earliest days of independent television in the fifties the individual companies had gone through perilous times. However, the second generation of regional franchise holders, Granada, Associated and Scottish, made large and rising profits, leading Lord Thompson of Scottish Television to declare his franchise 'a licence to print your own money'. When the time came for new franchises to be awarded by the Independent Television Authority in 1967, the reputation of the independent companies did not stand very high. Now new companies were formed, often associating themselves with individuals thought to have high cultural status. Meantime a couple of critical changes had taken place at the BBC. In 1960 Sir Hugh Greene, an upper-class figure, but one sensitive, like Trevelyan of the British Board of Film Censors, to changes taking place in society, became Director General of the BBC. In April 1964 the BBC's second channel, designed to develop the BBC's more serious output, came on the air.

From the very earliest days of radio British broadcasters had always been thoroughly aware of the looming presence of the United States. A strong conviction, which was only seriously been challenged in the 1980s, was that Britain must heed the awful warning of unrestrained commercialism, sponsored broadcasts and appeals to the lowest possible denominator. However, this conviction could coexist with the rational feeling that it was only sensible to learn from American technical innovations and from American talents in winning consenting audiences (this feeling greatly intensified during the Second World War). But finally, and most important, there was a profound consciousness of fundamental cultural differences between the two countries which required that British broadcasting should follow a British way: this is a view expressed quite clearly even by the advocates of commercial television in 1954.[11]

What I want to look at is the types of programme carried over from the fifties and at the changes of the middle sixties (almost entirely within the BBC). Where the BBC had panel games (*What's My Line?*, running from 1951 to 1963, was immensely popular), ITV had quizzes (with substantial prizes, something frowned upon by the BBC – most popular were *Take Your Pick* and *Double Your Money*). In July 1955 the BBC broadcast its first *This is Your Life*, a show which depended upon incredible planning and even more incredible deception to lure an unsuspecting celebrity into the studio to be presented with his life story. The BBC dropped the programme in 1964 (though ITV picked it up in 1969). It was in the very same month that the BBC began *Dixon of Dock Green*, the plodding police series which best encapsulates the naive pre-sixties television world. There had been a long-running controversy in BBC circles over whether (a) the British could make soap operas and (b) whether the British wanted soap operas. Associated Television came up with a winner – ITV's first twice-weekly serial – *Emergency-Ward 10*, about romantic entanglements rather than hospital emergencies. The young Albert Finney was an early 'patient'.[12] To Granada Television belongs the credit for the most clear-cut response to the new spirit stirring at the end of the fifties. *Coronation Street* was firmly set in the sort of traditional working-class streets celebrated by left-wing educationalist Richard Hoggart in his *The Uses of Literacy* (1957). Its cast consisted of obscure North Western repertory actors and its first episodes (beginning on Friday, 9 December 1960) were broadcast to local audiences only. From the following spring it was given national networking, and became a national institution. Its place in the context of this chapter is perfectly clear — its creator, twenty-three-year-old actor Tony Warren, has said: 'In 1960, the Northern resurgence was happening in the theatre and in films. I wanted to bring it to television. I wanted to see something written from the heart, acted by genuine Northerners.'[13]

There was, however, another aspect of television programming which relates integrally to the opening of this chapter and to the topic which will form its final section: programmes featuring the latest popular music. The protype was the BBC's *Six-five Special*, launched in 1957, and providing exposure for such performers as Adam Faith and Tommy Steele. *Juke Box Jury*, launched in June 1959, was based on the playing of new record releases. As a product of the major developments we have still to discuss, *Top of the Pops* (a programme based on record sales, but including a number of featured performers) went out for the first time on New Year's Day 1964. It had actually been preceded, by almost a year, by *Ready, Steady, Go!*, which had a whirlwind three-year career, bringing to fame a £10-a-week secretary and 'typical teenager', from Streatham, South London, Cathy McGowan.

There was a standard product of the British film industry usually catalogued as 'comedy', and usually of a rather low order. Television, as radio had long done, also essayed 'comedy'. The first comedy show to achieve critical as well as popular (an audience of 10 million) success was in fact a transfer from radio, *Hancock's Half-Hour*, scripted by Ray Galton and Alan Simpson.

In this study of culture (but not of broadcasting in general) two other fifties programmes need to be mentioned here. If one wanted to make the case for 1957 as a year of transition, one could stress that it was the year in which the photo-journalism magazine *Picture Post* folded and a revolutionary nightly television news magazine, *Tonight*, came into being. The other programme of note is *Monitor*, the first regular arts programme on television, introduced in 1958 and presented by Huw Wheldon, one of the great and the good in advanced cultural consensus; here the future film directors John

Schlesinger and Ken Russell gained their earliest experience.

By 1962 the liberalising influence of Sir Hugh Greene was beginning to be apparent. From the makers of *Tonight* there emerged the first ever programme genuinely satirizing current affairs, *That Was the Week That Was* (produced by Ned Sherrin, presented by David Frost). At the beginning of the same year, also on BBC, came *Z Cars*, the cops-and-robbers series set in a fictionalized Liverpool, which paid as much attention to the complexities and falliblity of the cops as it did to the excitements of detection and chase. Galton and Simpson came up with *Steptoe and Son*, the first of a genre in which comedy sprang out of character (in this case a culturally aspiring rag-and-bone man and his decrepit father), yet embraced issues which touched the feelings of intelligent audiences, while (of course) employing the street language which some still found shocking. The new genre achieved its ultimate form in *Till Death Us Do Part*, 'television's most controversial comedy series ever',[14] written by Johnny Speight, and featuring the ultra-conservative working man Alf Garnett, constantly in furious contention with his layabout, Labour-voting, son-in-law, and his stolid wife, Else. *Till Death Us Do Part* infuriated all opponents of the permissive society, though, with the delicious irony that lay at the core of the show; Alf Garnett himself was the most vociferous opponent of permissiveness. It was regularly viewed by over 17 million ordinary people, and was enthusiastically commented on by the critics.

The true location for, as it were, accommodation upon television of the sixties cultural revolution was the BBC's Wednesday Night Play. Nell Dunn was one of those upper-class young ladies who got swept up in Swinging London, who contributed to the new openness about female sexuality, and who took a genuine interest in working-class speech patterns. The title of her first novel, *Up the Junction* (1963), incorporates a bawdy pun connoting both pregnancy and the working-class South London area of Clapham Junction. Adapted as a Wednesday Play in 1965 it caused an outcry for its abortion scene (as a film, it was top money-maker of 1968). Another important Wednesday Play author was working-class, but Oxford-educated, Dennis Potter, whose *Vote, Vote, vote for Nigel Barton* took a working-class lad through Oxford into Labour politics. However, the sensation was *Cathy Come Home* (November 1966), written by Jeremy Sandford and directed by Ken Loach, the story of a young mother moving from one squalid lodging to another, then into a hostel for the homeless before finally being evicted and having her children taken away from her. Thus, the BBC had now established itself as the home of high-quality, 'serious' television, where in the seventies it was to be joined by certain of the ITV companies (though not before the over-ambitious London Weekend Television nearly went bankrupt and had to call upon capital from newspaper proprietor Rupert Murdoch). Internationally, what created the almost mythic status of British television was the BBC's last black-and-white drama series, *The Forsyte Saga* (1967), fashioned from the distinctly lower-middle-brow-novels of John Galsworthy, but with a brilliant cast of actors. Two years earlier commercial television had initiated what was to become a developing trend by bringing in the lurid American soap opera *Peyton Place*. All in all, by the early seventies, television was occupying the central cultural function served by film ten years earlier: it was, for instance, in 1973 that Stan Barstow's Yorkshire novel of 1964, *Joby*, finally reached the screen – the television screen.

While film suffered setbacks, television on the whole advanced in confidence and maturity. One of the best of all 'sit coms', embracing nostalgia without sentimentality, *Dad's Army*, was first presented on BBC in 1968, and grew in popularity, without loss of quality, throughout the seventies, thanks to the way in which scriptwriters David Croft and Jimmy Perry allowed situations to develop naturally, without ever forcing the humour. The BBC was also the home of a comedy series of an entirely different cast: *Monty Python's Flying Circus*, with its zany humour and appalling bad taste, held together by weird animations, was first presented in 1969. In 1971 London Weekend Television broadcast the first episodes of *Upstairs Downstairs*, a series based on the careful delineation of the hierarchy existing within an aristocratic Edwardian household, and, in international fame, the true successor to *The Forsyte Saga*. There were slightly grander ambitions on BBC2, which in the same year presented the six-part costume drama series *Elizabeth R*, starring Glenda Jackson. The *enfant terrible* of the sixties, Dennis Potter, showed his versatility in his series *Casanova*.

The basic concerns of television, in however traduced or modified form, are information and entertainment. In general, I have excluded from this book documentaries and other products relating essentially to information. However, the *World at War* series, directed by Jeremy Isaacs and presented by Thames Television in 1973, merits mention as marking a new standard in the handling of historical evidence on television.

Of entertainment television it would be fair to say that at its lowest, as in the highly popular games shows, British television was not quite as bad as it was in some other parts of the Western world, and that, at its basic lower-middle-brow level, it was a good deal better. Though there were many vacuous, fabricated, comedy shows, it was probably those comedy series which genuinely were funny which showed British television at its best: in 1975 there came *Fawlty Towers*, featuring John Cleese as the irascible hotel owner Basil Fawlty. But there was also, occasionally, serious drama of the very highest quality. Also in 1975 Thames Television put on the ninety-minute play *The Naked Civil Servant*, based on the autobiography of eccentric, but determined, homosexual Quintin Crisp, with John Hurt in the lead role: a play in which one laughed, and indeed sided, *with* such a character was a true sign of the maturity of British television, and a clear indication that it was preserving its own characteristics in face of American imports, of which the most important were the various American cops-and-robbers series, *Ironside*, *Kojak* etc. In the middle seventies came the first serious attempts at programmes catering for minority communities.

Popular music: the essence of the cultural revolution

In the developments discussed in this chapter so far, the working class (or substantial sections of it) were, as consumers, very important. On the production side a significant number of individuals from the working class (though they had usually risen through the educational system) made distinctive contributions as writers and, less often, directors. When we turn to pop music, the true essence of the cultural revolution, there is a case that this form originated largely from *within* the working class, in the sense that a generation of mainly working-class producers and consumers in the clubs and pubs seized on a variety of available musical materials and made them their own. But, of course, the working class was not an enclosed multitude, hermetically sealed from the rest of society: in technical colleges, art colleges, universities and even public schools young people plucked and yelled to the new skills. As the new music left its local audiences and became a vital component of the mass market, it inevitably slipped out of working-class hands.

The origins, anyway, lay solidly in America, with black rhythm and blues, transmitted to Britain by the white imitators and adaptors, principally Bill Haley and Elvis Presley. Since rhythm and blues connoted 'negro' music, the label used was 'rock 'n roll' which, ironically, in black American meant sexual intercourse. Haley's 'Rock Around the Clock' figured prominently in the American film *Blackboard Jungle* of 1955 and the record sold well in Britain at the end of that same year. In 1956 there arrived the film *Rock Around the Clock*; and in the year after that Bill Haley himself came on a British tour. The local, do-it-yourself, response came in the form of skiffle groups which ran in parallel with rock 'n roll, being widely regarded as a wholesome alternative to it. In Liverpool John Lennon (working-class) and Paul McCartney (lower middle-class) were captivated both by rock 'n roll and some of the black vocalists; in 1956 they were part of the Liverpool group The Quarrymen. In Newcastle Eric Burdon was imitating the blues singers, while in London Keith Richard modelled himself on the guitar-playing of such rock 'n roll stars as Chuck Berry.

By the end of the fifties there were at least 300 groups in Liverpool playing regularly in pubs, clubs, and dance halls. It was still all very localized, and even those with some sort of national reputation were scarcely lavishly rewarded, as is brought out in the story told to Michael Cable by guitarist Cockney Joe

Brown, who was so badly off on £15 per week that he had to go to work on the bus:

> It got really embarrassing in the end because I was supposed to be a bit of a star and people were recognising me from the telly and there I was scrabbling about on the bus with me guitars over one shoulder and me stage suit over the other. I had a helluva job getting one manager to let me have a cab from the station to the theatre on expenses. Even then it was only on condition that I got a receipt every time! Can you imagine asking a London cabbie for a receipt?! What's more, I was never allowed to give more than a threepenny tip.[15]

By 1960 Lennon and McCartney, together with George Harrison and Pete Best, had formed the beat group The Silver Beatles to play in such Liverpool clubs as the Cavern and the Jacaranda.

In many respects, pop music forms the perfect paradigm of culture as commodity constructed by the modern capitalist market. It is firmly based in technology, in particular electric (later electronic) amplification of the guitar (pioneered in America in the thirties). Even small-scale live performance required a certain amount of equipment; as pop moved from the cellars to the studios ever more sophisticated electronics came into play. For national and international success, a successful record was essential. All sorts of 'mediators' played their part in bringing about that initial success: the specialist press, particularly *New Musical Express* and *Melody Maker*; the compilers of hit parades — the two papers just mentioned continued to run their own even after the British Market Research Bureau top fifty was introduced in 1969; the producers and presenters of radio and television programmes; the agents and managers who constantly strove for ways of selling their 'properties' — the marketing, entertainment, non-musical, elements in pop help one in situating it very firmly at the entertainment end of the arts hierachy. Once performers were known through their hit records (and their occasional appearances on television), their live venues became vast arenas rather than intimate clubs.

None of that can rule out a role for genuine individual

talent; nor yet old-fashioned hard work and persistence. At the beginning of the sixties The Beatles, as they were now calling themselves, were big in Liverpool, but unknown elsewhere (they had spent a successful period in Hamburg). They had a most determined manager in Brian Epstein, who had a conception of how best to project the talents of wit and charm they possessed in addition to a certain musical inventiveness. Fresh mop-heads (rather than grease and sideburns) and suits, though suits without collars, gave a youthful but wholesome appearance. Five record companies turned the Beatles down (there were no local radio companies or local record companies) before Epstein persuaded EMI, where staff man George Martin did recognize the genuine musical skills of the group, to take them on. With the new drummer, Ringo Starr, 'Love Me Do' was recorded and released. It was a hit in the sense of making the lower reaches of the top twenty; 'Please, Please Me' which followed, reached second place. Epstein was then able to get EMI to take on several of the other south Lancashire groups he represented: the 'Mersey Sound' had arrived. But the Beatles were different, 'both as musicians with a thorough understanding of the culture from which they drew their style, and as people who were unlike entertainers previously familiar to audiences and journalist'.

The group's vocal style was a derivative of two American styles which had not previously been put together, the hard rock 'n' roll style like the singers Little Richard and Larry Williams, and the soft gospel co-and-response style of the Shirelles, the Drifters, and the rest of the singers produced by Leiber and Stoller, Luther Dixon, and Berry Gordy. Instrumentally, the Beatles were at first less inventive, producing a harsh rhythm and shrill sound comparable to some of the better American 'twist' records, including Bruce Channel's 'Hey! Baby' and Buster Brown's 'Fannie Mae'.

Although the twist had been fairly successful (without the impact it had in America), the gospel-harmony groups had very little success in Britain, and the result for the British audience was a sound with a familiar rhythm and a novel vocal style. The way the Beatles echoed one another's phrases, dragged out words across several beats, shouted 'yeah', and went into falsetto cries, was received in Britain as their own invention; it seemed that Britain had finally discovered an original, indigenous rock 'n' roll style. [16]

Gillett stresses that the Beatles themselves made no attempt to conceal their debt to American performers, but seems to underestimate the originality, both melodic and harmonic, of the Lennon–McCartney songs. The originality and simplicity appealed to British audiences: there followed 'From Me to You', 'She Loves You' and 'I want to Hold your Hand', which seemed to contrast with the lush contrivances of contemporary American records. Because they played their own instruments, and brought their own songs which they had usually tried out on live audiences, they were 'less subject to their producer than a studio group would have been'[17] – credit was due to George Martin for recognizing this and (in the early days) setting up arrangements which brought out the best in his performers.

When the first four records were released in America they met with no great success (Capitol, who had first option, allowed them to go to lesser companies). Intensive lobbying by Epstein, pressure from EMI and, Gillet reckons, the force of world opinion, led to Capitol itself putting heavy promotion behind 'I Want to Hold your Hand', which went to the top of the national charts. The earlier releases now enjoyed a tremendous revival, so that in March 1964 the Beatles held the top five places. The American tour of 1964 consolidated their position as the top pop group in the world. They continued to develop musically (assisted particularly between 1966 and 1968 by George Martin); they were both inventive and eclectic. *Sergeant Pepper's Lonely Hearts Club Band* (1967) 'revolutionized the record business by showing that an album offered artistic possibilities that could make it an alternative rather than a supplement to singles'.[18] It also symbolized that bridging of the chasm between 'art' and popular music, that softening of the snobbery that used to exist, to which the Beatles made a unique contribution: *Sergeant Pepper* 'is a dramatic cycle ... drawing in a full symphony as well as influences from Indian music'; among the heroes grouped in the photographic montage on the record sleeve is Stockhausen[19], unbending apostle of the sternest musical modernism. Then with the single 'Hey Jude' (1968) the Beatles created one of the most memorable of all popular songs. The wholesome image of the beginning of the decade was now submerged in that of 'flower power' and strong hints of drug culture. The Beatles broke up in 1969: in one sense they *were* the sixties.

The only true rivals to the Beatles were the London-based rhythm and blues group. The Rolling Stones who, by the deliberate decision of their manager Andrew Oldham, projected a consciously wild and anti-social image. They also came from a complete social class above the Beatles: when the group was founded, Mick Jagger, lead singer, was a student at the London School of Economics and two other members were at the Sidcup Art school. Oldham took them to America to record, and both their first British number one, 'It's All Over Now', and their first American top ten hit, 'Time is On My Side', were recorded in Chicago. Their most powerful records, from 1965 onwards, were made in the RCA studio in Hollywood: 'Satisfaction', 'Paint it Black', 'Honky Tonk Woman'.

By the end of the sixties, the Rolling Stones had virtually created a new category for themselves; having moved on from the Chuck Berry/Bo Didley/Muddy Walters Boogie Blues, through the soul influence of Solomon Burke and Don Covay, which represented the entire panorama of the past fifteen years of black dance music, they welded it all to lyrics which enabled a young white audience to identify themselves with the messages. And all this, while continuing to ignore 'the rules' by which popular entertainers traditionally found acceptance in the media. So far as anyone could tell from the outside, the Rolling Stones did not care what anyone thought about them, and this insolence gave them great strength.[20]

The British scene, it may be noted, was highly male-dominated: songs by male groups were often sexually extremely aggressive; songs by the relatively few female performers tended to be submissive in the traditional way. Most innovative was Dusty Springfield (her 'You Don't Have to Say you Love Me' was a huge international hit in 1966); Sandie Shaw was simply a very appealing singer of uncontroversial pop.

Pop music, in all its forms, was becoming (most markedly in the seventies) a massive international industry (though often, it should be noted, an insecure one, since record companies themselves were only minor components of big transnational corporations). The nature of popular music was irrevocably transformed and, for all the revivals and rebellions, continued along the same lines, with the great hits of the sixties as the constant points of reference, to at least the end of the eighties. By the beginning of the seventies British products had lost their dominant place in the American charts; and here there is space to do no more than to name some of the performers thought to have managed to preserve something distinctively personal, or British, amid the international tide.

The Who, aiming at something of the wild image of the Rolling Stones, were closely associated with the youth faction known as the Mods, but only achieved full international recognition with the first ever rock opera, *Tommy* (1969), put together by guitarist Pete Townshend. The Kinks had a series of eight top ten hits presenting, in the words of Gillett, 'cleverly drawn cartoon portraits of contemporary British life',[21] including 'Sunny Afternoon', 'Dead End Street' and 'Dedicated Follower of Fashion'. The Yardbirds, at their peak, were associated with the outstanding guitarist Eric Clapton. Clapton, a serious artist, left the group partly over what he took to be their brazen commercialism, and partly over his commitment to the blues. But in the world of pop it was very difficult to preserve a genuine 'alternative' or 'underground' identity. Gillett describes

a new underworld of basement cellars which sprang up during 1966 and 1967 as an alternative to the beer-and-cigarettes world of pubs and clubs that spawned the British blues groups. At the Middle Earth and UFO in London's West End, the audience took acid or smoked dope in the gloom, while a grandly-titled 'light show' projectionist lit up the wall at the back of the stage with oil-slides that stirred under the heat of his lamp. The erratic rhythms of the musicians threw the audience into spasm-dance movements, while the guitarist carried themselves off into space. This was the spirit of San Francisco, 6,000 miles East.[22]

From this world there emerged Pink Floyd, 'T. Rex' (Mark Bolan) and David Bowie, all of whom enjoyed considerable commercial success in the seventies. Bolan and Bowie, says Gillett, 'rekindled the spirit of teenage pop music': 'Presenting themselves with gaudy images decorated in lipstick, powder, and paint, they laid the foundation for a lively music scene in Britain, where most of the international innovators of the seventies were based.'[23]

Less innovative, but among the most popular performers throughout the seventies, and onwards, were Elton John, whose adaptive, eclectic talents enabled him in 1974 to sign a five-year contract guaranteeing him nearly £1 million per annum for records alone, it being estimated that in an eighteen-month period he could gross around £30 million,[24] and the Swedish group Abba, winners of the Eurovision Song Competition in that same year. Abba are important in a number of ways: contrasting with the classical sixties groups, they were essentially female-led ('Give Me a Man After Midnight' being one of their distinctive hits); giving very few live performances, they depended heavily on the latest technological gimmick, videos, for their exposure, apart, of course, from their reliance on the technology of the recording studio. Michael Cable, in a comment which sums up much of the nature of the entire industry, notes:

Their recording engineer discovered the 'secret' of the highly successful Abba sound purely by chance. He was messing about with his equipment when he realised that by double-tracking an instrument but at a different tape speed from the original recording it was possible to create the very full instrumental backing which has been the trademark of over £30 million-worth of record sales.[25]

Of course, many other groups, American and British, shared in the success of the two I have rather arbitrarily picked out. Pop had an enormous appeal, and many of its practitioners came from the upper levels of society. Together with, first, British film, and then British television, British pop music both earned international renown and worked changes within British society. Certainly dents had been made in the snobbery that used to exist. An alternative working-class culture had not replaced the upper- and middle-class culture of the forties and fifties: but there was in place a culture, enjoyed by all classes, in the creation of which the working class had at least played a part. But even that is an incomplete formulation. The advent of rock-based pop had been preceded by a jazz revival. The world of making and enjoying music now embraced jazz, 'folk' (of many kinds), rock and all types of classical music, 'early', 'middle' and 'late'. That world could not simply be mapped along lines of class:[26] the sources of cultural practice come from deep in the human spirit.

Notes

1 As quoted in Michael Cable, *The Pop Industry Inside Out* (1977), p. 13.
2 Seen by courtesy of that indefatiguable film historian, Dr Tony Aldgate. See in particular my '*Room at the Top*: the novel and the film' in the collection I edited on *The Arts, Literature and Society* (1990).
3 Quoted by John Hill, *Sex, Class and Realism: British Cinema 1956–1963* (1986), p. 86.
4 ibid., p. 196.
5 Alan Sillitoe's introduction to the 'Heritage of Literature' reprint of *Saturday Night and Sunday Morning* (1968), p. xii.
6 Interview with Harry Saltzman in *Kinematograph Weekly* (24 March 1960). For illuminating points on the making of the film see Alan Sillitoe 'What comes on Monday', *New Left Review*, July–August 1960, pp. 58–9 and Alexander Walker, *Hollywood England: the British Film Industry in the Sixties* (1974), pp. 80–91.
7 See the excellent chapter on this film by Jeffrey Richards in *Best of British: Cinema and Society 1930–1970*, by Jeffrey Richards and Anthony Aldgate (1983).
8 Roy Armes, *A Critical History of the British Cinema* (1978), pp. 317–18.
9 Andrew J. Edelstein, *The Swinging Sixties* (New York, 1986), pp. 140–41.
10 Ibid., p. 124.
11 All of this emerges strongly from the four volumes of *The History of Broadcasting in the United Kingdom* (1961–2) by Asa Briggs. The basic points are brilliantly developed by Valeria Camporesi in her doctoral dissertation, 'Mass culture and the defense of national

traditions: the BBC and American Broadcasting, 1922–1954' (European University Institute, Florence, 1990).

12 Hilary Kingsley and Geoff Tibballs, *Box of Delights: the Golden Years of Television* (1989), p. 33. I have depended heavily on this most useful book.

13 Quoted in Kingsley and Tibballs, ibid., p. 55.

14 Ibid., p. 87.

15 Cable, *The Pop Industry*, p. 8.

16 Charlie Gillett, *The Sound of the City* (rev. edn., 1983), p. 263. See also Richard Middleton, *Pop Music and the Blues* (1972), especially pp. 167–4, 182–4, 233–5. In general, see Hunter Davies, *The Beatles: the Authorised Biography* (1968); Dave Laing, *The Source of Our Time* (1969); Wilfrid Mellers, *Twilight of the Gods: the Beatles in Retrospect* (1973).

17 Gillett, *Sound of the City*, p. 264.

18 Cable, *The Pop Industry*, p. 10.

19 Paul Griffiths 'Music', in *The Cambridge Guide to the Arts in Britain: Since the Second World War* (ed. Boris Ford, 1988), p. 80.

20 Gillett, *Sound of the City*, p. 270.

21 Ibid., p. 276.

22 Ibid., p. 397.

23 Ibid., p. 399.

24 Cable, *The Pop Industry*, p. 122.

25 Ibid., p. 86.

26 See Ruth Finnegan's study of music-making in Milton Keynes, *The Hidden Musicians: Music-making in an English Town* (Cambridge, 1989).

9 Art: Modernist Programmes and Personal Visions

Of all institutions of higher education in the sixties, art colleges were the most mixed in social composition. But while 'democratic' influences were strong, so also were those counsels which declare that the art of our era must be modernist and that modernism itself must be a relentless forward march. The art of the sixties comprised both the work of modernist radicals and of individualists (of whom the best known is David Hockney) who saw no need whatever to conform to modernist manifestos. A key event in the evolution of modernism had occurred as far back as 1917 when Marcel Duchamp signed the name R. Mutt on an ordinary urinal and exhibited it as *Fountain*. One of the characteristics of modernism is its self-consciousness about art: here Duchamp was, in a highly mischievous way, raising questions about the very nature of art; it is, as we know, part of contemporary cultural theory to question the whole idea of art as separate from other social practices. And if there has been one universal trend in recent aesthetic and intellectual endeavour it is towards perceiving all activities and exchanges as 'language.'

Since recent American studies of British sculpture have identified 'a quiet revolution' commencing around 1965[1], I shall begin with sculpture, though, in my view, sculpture continued to exhibit that process of continuous successive reactions against the older generation already mentioned rather than any distinctive 'revolution'. One must start with Anthony Caro (b. 1924), since the end of the fifties one of the most influential figures in the British art world, who certainly went through something of a personal 'revolution'. Educated at upper-

Plate 3   Anthony Caro, *Twenty-four Hours* (1960). Sculpture: oil on
metal 1384 × 2235 × 838 mm. Acknowledgments to the
artist and the Tate Gallery.

class Charterhouse and Christ's College Cambridge, Caro subsequently studied at the (much lower-class) Regent Street
Polytechnic and the (relatively classless) Royal Academy schools.
His apprenticeship as a sculptor was served between 1951 and
1953 as an assistant to Henry Moore. Then in 1959 he visited
the United States where he fell under the influence of the
critic Clement Greenberg, the apostle of Abstract Expressionism
as the 'post-painterly' culmination of modernism. Back in Britain
the following year, Caro manifested a radical reaction against
both the monumentality of Moore and the spindly figurism of
Butler, in his *Twenty-four hours*, an abstract construction in
painted sheet metal, which consciously attempted to replicate
the flatness of the kind of painting Greenberg was promoting
(plate 3). The first public exhibition of his welded metal constructions, sometimes covered in brilliant household paint so
that the metal appeared weightless as plastic or fibreglass,[2]
took place at the Whitechapel Gallery in 1963. Caro had a
two-day-a-week teaching post at the St Martin's School of Art,

where he exerted a very powerful influence (characteristically of the medium, as much by reaction as by example) over what came to be known as the 'New Generation' group of sculptors (the name given to the group exhibition held at the Whitechapel Art Gallery in 1965). Fuller puts it sourly, if wittily:

Caro had declared that sculpture could be anything; but his rebellious pupils took him more literally than he intended. Barry Flanagan and Nicholas Pope reduced the art to placement of barely worked materials. Others started digging holes, taking photographs, and even walks, and calling that sculpture too.[3]

A kind of transition point may be detected in 'Sculpture: Open Air Exhibition of Contemporary British and American Works', at Battersea Park in 1963. Among the American exhibitors was the leading exponent of abstract assemblages, David Smith. At the 'Sculpture in the Open Air' exhibition of 1966, also in Battersea Park, attention focused on Caro and his younger followers. The exhibition was in some sense a homage to David Smith, now dead: his was the only American work in what was essentially a British exhibition.

In the international art world there developed the notions of Conceptual Art, Earthwork and Arte Povera. What happened, in fact, was that as well as an explosion in what was considered to be art, there was an abandonment of distinctions between 'sculpture' and 'painting'. We must therefore look at certain developments in the realm of painting; we must go back to the 'Place' exhibition organized at the ICA in 1959 by Robyn Denny (b. 1930), Richard Smith (b. 1931) and Ralph Rumney. In Spalding's words: 'Large, human-sized canvases of standardised dimensions and colours (red, green, white and black) were arranged to form corridors and vistas. The intention was to create a total environment, to give the visitor the sensation of being inside a space generated by the colours.'[4] Just as there were new film production companies and new provincial theatres, this group of artists hoped to by-pass the dealer system. Denny organized two 'Situation' exhibitions in 1960 and 1961. The St Ives artists were deliberately excluded, the aim being to publicize large-scale, and usually 'hard-edge', abstracts ('hard-edge' abstraction, associated with such American artists as

Kenneth Noland, attempts to achieve a geometrical precision with a knife-sharp contour, the 'hard edge').

Across the plastic arts radicals began to concentrate on two interlinked ideas: that art should be stripped down to its essentials, giving rise to Minimal Art; that art should be refined down to its fundamental definition or basic idea, giving rise to Conceptual Art. In Coventry (initiatives from the provinces are important in all of the cultural developments of the sixties) a group of 'Minimalists', Terry Atkinson, David Bainbridge, Michael Baldwin and Harold Hurrell, founded the *Journal of Art and Language* group. In May 1969 *Art and Language 1* was published with the subtitle 'the Journal of Conceptual Art' (though this designation was dropped in subsequent issues). The Art and Language Group brought together such diverse figures as Gilbert and George, Keith Arnatt (b. 1930) and Charles Harrison. What is generally reckoned the first Conceptual Art exhibition, 'When Attitudes become form', took place at the ICA from August to September 1969, having first toured mainland Europe. In 1970 Charles Harrison organized the exhibition 'Idea Structures' at the Camden Arts Centre. Taking Minimalism to the ultimate by pursuing as a theme the possible disappearance of art and the artist, Keith Arnatt sent to this exhibition an essay entitled 'is it possible for me to do nothing as my contribution to the exhibition'.[5] The most obvious characteristic of Conceptual Art was the incorporation in it of not just words, but whole sentences, and even paragraphs. In 1972 Keith Arnatt exhibited 'a wall inscription' at the Tate Gallery: it was literally that, the words KEITH ARNATT IS AN ARTIST printed on to the wall. Most enduring of the conceptual artists has been Michael Craig-Martin whose famous *An Oak Tree* of 1973 is actually a glass of water high up on a glass shelf — an art object is what the artist says it is.

As in other spheres in the sixties, there a strong 'democratic' motivation: art should not be élitist, art should not been seen as something permanent and above the temporal limitations of ordinary life; while art was being stripped down (which did seem to have rather élitist implications) it should also reach out into other spheres. Thus there was Temporal Art (constructions to be dismantled after being viewed),

Performance Art and Happenings (linking with drama, but also being evanescent), and Earth Art (which includes Installation, Land, and site-specific art, and in which parts of the landscape itself, 'straight', or perhaps with trenches dug in it, were declared also to be 'art').

Among British exhibitors at the 'When Attitudes become Form' exhibition had been Barry Flanagan and Richard Long. Around 1966–7, Flanagan, born in Wales in 1941, was creating coloured Hessian sacks filled with paper, foam, or sand – variously described as Process Art, Anti-form, or Postminimalist. He then became involved in Temporal Art. Richard Long, born in Bristol in 1945, is one of the leading British figures in the international Earth Art movement: Long presented maps and photographs of landscape as well as arrangements of gathered stones. Third in the trio of leading 'New Generation' sculptors is Tony Cragg. Born in Liverpool in 1949, Cragg trained as a scientist, and in 1968–69 was working as a research associate in a biochemistry laboratory carrying out experiments on natural rubber. He enrolled in the Gloucester College of Art, subsequently moving to the Wimbledon School of Art. Cragg saw art 'as an expansion of his interest in science: to Cragg, both science and art deal with ideas, the former taking an abstract form, the latter a tangible one.'[6] By the mid seventies (he was to change later) Cragg was firmly associated with Temporal Art – producing a series of stacks which could readily be dismantled. In its annual exhibition of 1972 the Arts Council displayed the range of 'arts' and 'isms' under the not very original title of 'The New Art'. Hostility to what of all blind alleys appeared most blind broke into the open in 1976 when there was a perhaps too carefully orchestrated outcry over the exhibiting at the Tate of *Equivalent VIII* by the American minimalist and conceptual sculptor Carl Andre. The work actually dated back to 1966 and had been acquired by the Tate in 1972, and twice exhibited before 1976 – to its supporters it was an orderly arrangement of fire-bricks.

Gilbert (b. 1943) and George (b. 1942) were still sculpture students at the St Martin's School of Art when they attracted international attention for a peculiar and highly personal twist on the notions of art as 'performance' and as being 'temporal':

in what was first called 'Our new Sculpture', then 'Underneath the Arches' and, finally, 'The Singing Sculpture', they themselves posed as their own 'sculptures'. The next stage was to seek a permanent form for these 'living sculptures': 'they began to use the traditional media of painting and drawing, in a novel and witty way, creating numerous 'drawing pieces', 'charcoal on paper sculptures' and one huge 'painting sculpture', in all of which the posed image of the artists appears life-size.[7]

In 1971, they turned to photography, creating the 'photo-piece' which, henceforth, was to be the basic form of their art.

The photo-piece consists basically of an arrangement of a number of separately framed photographic images adding up to a unified expressive whole. The photographs themselves are manipulated in various ways through the printing process to enhance their expressive potential and in the early photo-pieces the framed images were hung in configurations which were emblematic of the theme of the piece[8]

Words and phrases often appear on these photo-pieces, seeming to maintain a link with Conceptual Art: but Gilbert and George saw themselves as 'New Realists'. From 1973 there was an emphasis on urban settings: many appeared to be about drinking and drunkenness – in his note for the 1986 retrospective exhibition Simon Smith explained this as being 'a particularly apt metaphor to express what was clearly a state of considerable alienation and existential angst which gripped them at that time.'[9]

Four notable artists (two female, two male – Elisabeth Frink, Bridget Riley, David Hockney and Ron Kitaj) stand apart from the developments I have just been discussing. Frink (b. 1930) was the youngest of the generation of sculptors (Chadwick, Meadows, Armitage, Butler, Puoalozzi and Caro) following that of Moore and Hepworth, but the sources of her inspiration were her Catholic faith and internationalist political commitment, and her fascination with strange beasts and birds (see Plate 4), with horses, and with the male figure in various situations; she owned to a life-long obsession with the theme of the Four Horsemen of the Apocalypse. Her preferred way of

Plate 4 Elisabeth Frink, *Harbinger Bird IV* (1960). Sculpture: bronze. 483 × 213 × 356 mm. Acknowledgments to the artist and the Tate Gallery.

working was 'in very wet plaster, working fast, smoothing the surface, letting it dry, altering it and breaking it up, doing it again until all forms became simplified, straightened out, details eliminated'.[10] The sculpture would then be cast in bronze, sometimes in several copies. In 1972, at the beginning of the great feminist era partly inspired by Germaine Greer's *The Female Eunuch* (1970), fellow artist Sir Edwin Mullins could declare that Frink's beasts, birds or human males all represented 'the dominant male ... aggressive, mindless, physical and predatory'.[11] Frink herself has offered a less stereotyped account:

My sculptures of the male figure are both man and mankind. In these two categories are all the sources of all my ideas for the human figure. Man, because I enjoy looking at the male body and this has always given me and probably always will, the impetus and the energy for a purely sensuous approach to sculpture form. I like to watch a man walking and swimming and running and being . . . I can sense in a man's body a combination of strength and vulnerability – not as weakness but as the capacity to survive through stoicism or passive resistance, or to suffer or feel. My earlier sculptures of men in the fifties and sixties were a combination of men at war, for instance, the bird men; the spinning men, men in flight; and men in space . . . my earlier figures were not at all sensuous: they were too much involved with fractured wings or the debris of war and heroics. By this last phrase I mean individual courage.[12]

Frink also explained that the series of goggle heads of the later sixties were a 'symbol of evil and destruction', referring to Moroccan policies in North Africa. The running men and figures which followed related to her political preoccupation with human rights world-wide.[13] If anything Frink's development was towards naturalism, as can be seen in *Man* (1970), 'totally contained within himself.[14] In all her art she is toughly and uncompromisingly female (rather than feminine – or even feminist).

Bridget Riley (b. 1931), the leading British exponent of what became known as Op Art, took some time to find the artistic language through which to express that which she felt she had to express: according to the sympathetic account by Sir John Rothenstein she remained oblivious to contemporary continental and American optical art, the main influences on her being Seurat, the Italian futurists, and the black-and-white early Renaissance architecture of Pisa, all studied in the summer of 1960. The *Pink Landscape* which she did soon afterwards was based on 'the experience of a stretch of landscape in the hills south of Siena, drenched in a blinding shimmering heat-haze that ended in one of the fiercest storms of that summer', but it already shows that concern 'with a kind of optical situation which constantly recurs in her later work – that of a dominant formal pattern under pressure of disintegration'.[15] Riley's description of herself as 'just the agent' caught up in her medium is reminiscent of Francis Bacon's expression of his artistic vocation, though otherwise the artists are totally different. Riley felt that she needed to exercise control: 'One can easily be overwhelmed, carried away.' Thus her mature works are preceded by large numbers of preparatory studies, the final work actually being made by skilled assistants, a practice she has justified as follows: 'I need assistants for speed's sake: before one painting is done I have ideas for others (in any case I work on several at once). Without help I would be frustratingly held up.[16] Her first utterly characteristic work was *Movement in Squares* (1961, tempera on board) which, in the words of Rothenstein:

clearly expresses one of the principal subjects of her art, namely the interaction of opposing elements: stability and movement, discord and harmony, constancy and change, passivity and energy, light and darkness, advance and recession, ease and tension, repose and disturbance. 'Movement in Squares' shows the gradual compression of the central squares into rectangles by those to the left and right, and the resulting contrast between the solid, regular and compressed squares. The visual experience thus generated is one of dynamic contrasts.[17]

Riley's intention was to administer an 'electric shock' (again one is reminded of Bacon) through her resolution of tension between active and static and other conflicting forces and states of mind. Her earlier works are entirely in black and white, as for instance *Fall* (1963, emulsion on board), which was included in her second exhibition at Gallery One in 1963. The Introduction to the catalogue said this:

We are faced with an inexorable yet almost imperceptible variation of linear elements and units. So smooth is the change that it does not allow the eye to organise the series of units into stable, larger entities in which it might linger and rest. There is a constant tug-of-war between shifting and crumbling patterns, but at a certain point this relentless attack on our lazy viewing habits peels our eyes into a new and crystal clear sensibility.[18]

After studio experiments with colour, Riley began to introduce a variety of greys in 1965 and then finally pure colour, as in *Late Morning* (1968, emulsion).

David Hockney, a lower-middle-class boy from Bradford, a vegetarian and conscientious objector, was born in 1937. He took to etching at college because he could not afford the materials for painting, visited New York on £100 he had managed to save, and produced the series of etchings, *The Rake's Progress*, which made him £5,000 while still a student. Hockney differs radically from the radicals I discussed in the first part of this chapter in that he did not share the view that not only did one have to be relentlessly modern but that one must relentlessly advance to further stages of modernism. An important part of Hockney's strength was his complete emancipation from the theories about the nature of art, about Marxism, about structuralism, and post-structuralism, and about language which so obsessed so many of his contemporaries. The major influence on him, in fact, came very early, from a fellow student at the Royal College of Art, R. G. Kitaj, an American who had already experienced the real world as sailor and the soldier. Kitaj, a much more cerebral personality (discussed in a moment) extended Hockney's knowledge of contemporary painting and directed him towards portraying whatever most deeply stirred his interest. Hockney was quickly to develop an eclecticism and inventiveness reminiscent, at times, of Picasso; he drew upon Pop Art, incorporated photographic images, switched from oil paint to acrylic, rejected the fashionable contempt for the pretty, and evinced a mighty disrespect for the canons of wisdom handed down in the colleges. In a conversation with Peter Webb, Hockney remarked:

I have always been aware that there is a great pleasure in seeing. I tend to make things charming because that's my way, but often it's a bit of a disguise. I'm not afraid if they are pretty, I like pretty pictures. I tend to think that my view of the world is a bit oriental — I share their view of the tragic. Tragedy is a literary concept, not a visual one.[19]

Earlier he had said:

I have stopped bothering about modern art, in that at one time you would be frightened of doing things in painting because you would consider them almost reactionary. I've stopped believing that it's possible for art to progress only in a stylistic way.[20]

The very titles are expressive of his perhaps excessively eclectic early style: *A Grand Procession of Dignitaries in the Semi-Egyptian Style* (1961, oil); *We Two Boys Clinging Together* (1961, oil); *Tea Painting in an Illusionistic Style* (1962, oil). The individualistic, personal, style became apparent in the two oils of 1963 'The First Marriage' (Plate 5) and 'The Second Marriage'. Hockney explained the origins of the 'Marriage' paintings as being a sudden perception, in profile, of a friend standing in a Berlin museum.

Plate 5 David Hockney, *The First Marriage* (1963). Oil on canvas. 1829 × 2140 mm. Acknowledgments to the artist, Tradhart, and the Tate Gallery.

To one side of him, also in profile, was a sculpture in wood of a seated woman of a heavily stylized kind (Egyptian, I believe). For a moment they seemed together − like a couple posing. At first I was amused at the sight of them together; but later I made some drawings incorporating both my friend and the sculpture. When I returned to London I decided to use the drawings to make a painting ... I called it 'The Marriage' because I regarded it as a sort of marriage of styles. The heavily stylized female figure with the not so stylized 'bridegroom'. On completing this picture I decided to do another version of the same theme ... Taking the idea of marriage literally I decided to put them in a definite setting – a domestic interior.[21]

Hockney travelled all over the world, absorbing all kinds of influences, but, by his own declaration, it is Southern California which has influenced him most: 'When I flew over San Bernardino and looked down and saw the swimming pools of the houses, I was more thrilled than I had ever been arriving at any other city.[22] Hockney went on experimenting and developing; he tried his hand (as had Picasso) at theatrical design. In his openness, his spontaneity, his indifference to received dogma, and his flamboyant demonstrations of practice triumphing over preaching, he was *the* painter of sixties Britain, though one with a continuing and developing reputation throughout the seventies and the eighties.

R. G. Kitaj was born in Cleveland, USA, as Ronald Brooks; his later name came from his mother's second husband, an Austrian refugee and research chemist, Dr Walter Kitaj. Possessed of enormous personal dynamism, Kitaj tried his hand as a sailor as well as a painter before doing national service in the US army. In 1957 he began to study art in Oxford, and in 1960 he entered the Royal College of Art where he struck up his portentous friendship with Hockney, while at the same time developing a deep personal interest in twentieth-century poetry, particularly American. Between 1961 and 1967 he had teaching posts at the Ealing Technical College, the Camberwell School of Art, and the Slade School. In late 1979, Kitaj told the art critic Joe Shannon that he 'would like to do visually what modern poetry has done verbally – to make works as difficult, as multilevelled, as tough, and as full of human purport as a work by T. S. Eliot or Ezra Pound'.[23] The engagement with intellectual and moral issues can be seen in the very earliest paintings, such as *Erasmus* (1958), as well as in those of the sixties and seventies: for example, *The Ohio Gang* (1964), *If Not, Not* (1975–6) – which well exemplifies Shannon's statement that 'Kitaj's best works don't spell out specific events so much as create an atmosphere of social calamity'[24] – *Sighs from Hell* (1979), an understated, non-horrific group of girls in pastel and charcoal on paper, and *The Rise of Fascism* (1979).

Older artists, of course, such as Bacon, Freud, Auerbach, and Kossoff, and the pop artists introduced above in chapter 4, continued in business. Of the newer work, the key concept which links it to the other aspects of the cultural revolution is 'liberation'. It took very different forms, but then 'doing your own thing' was also a key notion of the sixties. Caro liberated his followers into what some would see as an élitist sterility; Hockney, who appeared more conventional, was the very voice of liberation; Gilbert and George became the darlings of middle-brow taste.

Notes

1 Terry A. Neff (ed.), *A Quiet Revolution: British Sculpture since 1965* (1987).
2 Peter Fuller, 'The Visual Arts', in *The Cambridge Guide to the Arts in Britain: since the Second World War* (ed. Boris Ford, 1988), p. 138.
3 Ibid., p. 139.
4 Frances Spalding, *British Art since 1900*, p. 189.
5 Ibid., p. 215.
6 Mary Jane Jacob, 'Tony Cragg: "first order experiences"', in Neff, *Quiet Revolution*, p. 54.
7 *Gilbert and George: Pictures 1982–86* (Hayward Gallery, 1986).
8 Ibid.
9 Ibid. In general see *Gilbert and George: the Complete Pictures 1971–1985* (1986).
10 Edwin Mullins, in *The Art of Elisabeth Frink* (1972), p. 6.
11 Ibid., p. 4.
12 *Elisabeth Frink Sculpture: Catalogue Raisonné* (1984), pp. 36–7.
13 Ibid., pp. 37–40.
14 Ibid., p. 37.
15 These quotations are cited by John Rothenstein, *Modern English Painters: Wood to Hockney* (1974), p. 215.

16 Ibid., pp. 217, 219.
17 Ibid., p. 216.
18 Quoted in ibid., p. 216.
19 Peter Webb, *Portrait of David Hockney* (1988), p. 244.
20 Rothenstein, *Modern English Painters*, p. 230.
21 Quoted in ibid., p. 227.
22 Quoted in ibid., p. 228.
23 John Ashberry, Joe Shannon, Jane Livingstone and Timothy Hyman, *Kitaj: Paintings, Drawings, Pastels* (1983), p. 18.
24 Ibid., p. 17.

10 Underground and Overground

The cultural practices discussed in chapter 8 did involve the masses of the population. The practices discussed in chapter 9 were largely minority ones. 'Swinging London', connoting the highly publicized carryings-on of the beautiful, the wealthy, and the successful, was confined (though 'permissiveness' spread much more widely) to an exceptional few; so was what was variously described as 'the underground' or 'the counter-culture'. The theorists of the counter-culture claimed that it would overthrow dominant 'bourgeois' culture, creating a society in which the masses would be liberated. They failed to notice that liberation was already taking place.

The organs of the underground were *International Times* (*IT*, founded in October 1966), *Oz* (founded February 1967) and *Friends* (later *Frendz*, founded November 1969). The concerns of the underground were Love, Dope and Rock (very much the concerns, indeed, of Swinging London). Love meant sex, and rather crudely male chauvinist sex at that: pornography was a standard ingredient in underground magazines; the advocacy of explicit sexual scenes on the stage formed a link to the somewhat ambiguously placed 'alternative theatre' (see below). Drugs were held to be mind-expanding: the new enlightenment they would bring would entail both universal peace and revolution. *Friends* began as *essentially* a rock magazine and, as *Frendz*, finished as *largely* a rock magazine; rock was much discussed in the other magazines. Here was another link to the (changing) culture I have already described; Pink Floyd, as we saw, emerged from the underground to achieve commercial success in the seventies; Paul McCartney came to the massive 'launch party' of *International Times* (dressed as an Arab!); so did Antonioni and his leading actress Monica Vitti.[1] The slitheriness of the whole notion of a counter-culture is exposed still further by the rock festivals represented as being a significant constituent of it. The biggest British one took place on the Isle of Wight in 1970: there was a VIP enclosure protected by guards, while many fans could not afford the admission price, let alone the food prices. *IT*'s music writer Mick Farren wrote that the festival illustrated 'a culture which, although paying lip-service to the concepts of love and equality, manifests an inequality of rank and money as brutal as that of czarist Russia'.[2] It is only fair to add that the earlier free festivals in Hyde Park did more genuinely express 'the concepts of love and equality'.

After rock, the second most important interface between underground and 'straight' culture lay in the theatre. At the very heart of alternative theatre were small agit-prop companies with no fixed abode, and also Charles Marowitz's 'Theatre of Cruelty' in London. Next were the new, small, 'experimental' theatres, such as the Traverse in Edinburgh, then the established, and subsidized, provincial companies, such as the Bristol Old Vic, the Coventry Belgrade, the Glasgow Citizens', and the Nottingham Playhouse. In a position of its own stood London's Royal Court. The complication was that the highly prestigious national companies, subsidized by the authorities the underground was aiming at overthrowing, and even the commercial theatres, began presenting 'alternative' plays, while the experimental theatres began to get subsidies from both local authorities and direct from the Arts Council. It is true that the Traverse theatre did sometimes fall foul of the rather puritan Edinburgh town council, but basically the Traverse, with its restaurant, bar and art gallery, was a cultural arm of upper-middle-class Edinburgh. If, for 'underground', with its subversive implications, or 'counter-culture', invoking the mirage of the dialectic, we substitute 'bohemia' we have a juster measure of its political and social significance; for the whole wonderful world of theatrical innovation the word 'fringe' serves very well.

There was another interface in the practice of poetry: among other things underground poetry aimed to break down the élitist barriers surrounding this art form, particularly through poetry readings. Though questions may be posed as to whether serious poetry does not really have to be puzzled out on the printed page, and whether poetry made for declamation may not confuse rhetoric with genuine poetic effect, I should add immediately that 'the Liverpool Poets' have their honoured section in Edward Lucie-Smith's *British Poetry since 1945*, the standard work which I have already cited several times. Some of the Liverpool poets were painters, one, Adrian Henri (b. 1932), was, like many of the artists I discussed in the previous chapter, very much a self-conscious thinker about the nature of modernism, with an interest in multi-media art and performance. Roger McGough (b. 1937) was a member of the satirical pop group The Scaffold; most were linked to the Mersey music scene, though the allegiance of Henry Graham (b. 1930) was, in fact, to jazz. Brian Patten (b. 1946), the youngest, stood somewhat apart, seeing poetry as 'nothing to do with education or saying anything'.[3] W. E. Parkinson writing on 'Poetry in the North East', does not rate highly the best known of the North East poets, such as Tom Pickard, and Barry MacSweeney.[4]

So far, I have very much looked at literature and drama as service trades to the cinema. Drama is the best medium for examining the way in which, in the sixties, audiences were integrating and re-forming. A survey of theatre audiences carried out in the spring of 1965 indicated the following: of male attenders 60.5 per cent came from the professional classes (amounting to no more than 7.5 per cent of the population as a whole): 11.7 per cent were teachers, 19.1 per cent in managerial positions, 15.9 per cent clerical and sales staff, and only 4.6 per cent blue-collar workers. Of female attenders, 22.8 per cent were teachers, 35 per cent clerical, 20.1 per cent students, 16.2 per cent housewives, 1.9 per cent saleswomen. Ronald Hayman concludes wisely that theatre audiences were not only unrepresentative of British society, they were unrepresentative even of the middle class. There were, he adds, different audiences for different types of theatre.[5] Most financially successful were musicals, thrillers and light comedies.[6] Such shows could expect to run for well over 250 performances, with the lower-middle-brow comedies *Boeing-Boeing* and *There's a Girl in my Soup* having over 2,000. In November 1972 box office records were broken by a further three light comedies: *Lloyd George Knew my Father*, by William Douglas Home, *The Mating Game*, by Robin Hawden, and *The Man Most Likely To*, by Joyce Rayburn. There were revivals of the classics, dramatized novels and many plays set in the past. Among new plays by new writers which managed, at least, more than 250 performances, Ronald Hayman lists: *Loot*, presented at the Royal Court in 1967, written by Joe Orton (1933–67), writer of strikingly original black farces, including *Entertaining Mr Sloane* (1964) and *What the Butler Saw* (1969); *The Killing of Sister George*, by Frank Marcus; *The Boys in the Band*, by Mark Crowley; the American import *Who's Afraid of Virginia Woolf?*, the highly explicit portrayal of a husband and wife tearing each other apart, which became the basis of the Hollywood movie generally regarded as marking the arrival of American films into the adult world of the sixties; *The Caretaker*, by Harold Pinter; *Luther*, by John Osborne – helped towards commercial success, Hayman suggests, because it featured a celebrated actor, Albert Finney; *Inadmissible Evidence* by the same author, and with another of the famous 'new' actors of the sixties, Nicol Williamson; *The Private Ear*, by Peter Shaffer; *The Public Eye*, also by Shaffer, with the much-admired Maggie Smith; *Chips with Everything*, by Arnold Wesker; *The Contractor*, by David Storey; *Spring and Port Wine*, by Bill Naughton; *The Ratte of a Simple Man*, by Charles Dyer; *Billy Liar*, by Keith Waterhouse; *40 Years On*, by the most consistent of the satirical writers of the time, Alan Bennett, with one of the acting giants, Sir John Gielgud.[7] Considerable commercial success was also achieved by Tom Stoppard (born in Czechoslovakia in 1937), writer of, in sparklingly witty paradoxical language, philosophical puzzles on questions of time and identity: *Rosencrantz and Guildenstern are Dead* of 1966, *The Real Inspector Hound* of 1968, *Jumpers* of 1972, and *Travesties* of 1974.

Justly famous, though not quite so outstandingly commercially successful, were David Rudkin (*Afore Night Come* of 1962 being accounted an early example 'Theatre of Cruelty'); Peter Nichols (b. 1927), author of *Day in the Death of Joe Egg* (1967), a bitter-sweet comedy about the bringing up of a severely handicapped child; Edward Bond (b. 1935), Marxist in politics, distinguished for his austere, polished dialogue and calculated employment of scenes of extreme cruelty — *Saved* (1965), *Narrow Road to the Deep North* (1968), *Bingo* (1974); David Halliwell (b. 1936), whose *Little Malcolm and his Struggle against the Eunuchs*, presented in 1965 at the tiny Lyric, Hammersmith, was the kind of 'alternative theatre' which attracted a respectable professional audience; and Christopher Hampton (b. 1946), launched on a career in both alternative and straight theatre with *When did you Last see my Mother*, of 1967). (Serious minority theatre — Shaw, Chekhov, Ibsen — I should stress, dated back to the Edwardian era.)

Thus a good slice of theatre was closely related to the leading cultural developments I discussed in chapter 8. But the point I am really concerned to make is that for consistently commercially successful theatre there was a minority audience which cannot be seen as representing any kind of dominant ideology but which, rather, was a kind of throw-back to earlier times. 'It is clear,' Hayman commented in 1973,

that much of the major successes are scored by shows that do not make any serious comment on the contemporary situation. One of the undeniable functions of the London theaatre is to cater for the appetite of old and middle-aged people for reminders of the elegance and glamour they remember or think they remember from time they were young[8]

At times, getting on for 50 per cent of these 'old and middle-aged people' were American tourists seeking a simply assimilated traditional British culture.[9]

In the seventies the plays which most notably combined critical acceptance with commercial success were the contemporary satires written by, for example, John Wells, and by Alan Ayckbourn. Ayckbourn made his way via the Library Theatre, Scarborough, but yet had a touch of Terence Rattigan about him: educated at the prestigious public school, Haileybury, his entrée to the theatre had been provided by a schoolmaster there. *Relatively Speaking* was a hit in the West End in 1967.

His treatment of the pomposities, foibles, snobbishness and minor cruelties of various sorts of middle-class people, combined with imaginative staging, established him as a leading playwright. *Absurd Person Singular* started in Scarborough in June 1972, and was presented in London's West End in July 1973; *Absent Friends* started in Scarborough in June 1974 and appeared in the West End in July 1975; *Bedroom Farce*, in which the three bedrooms of three cunningly contrasting couples were presented simultaneously on the stage, took from a Scarborough launch in June 1975 till March 1977 to make it to London, but this time with the special cachet of production by Peter Hall at the subsidized National Theatre. His success continued and multiplied throughout the eighties.

By the beginning of the sixties a new novel by Kingsley Amis was treated by the posh Sunday papers as a major literary event: as social structure and sexual morality shifted so did Amis's witty chronicles of his time; between *Take a Girl like You* (1960), wherein Jenny Bunn preserves her virginity through-out almost all of the novel, and *I Want it Now* (1968), the unambiguous sentiment of the leading, and very youthful, female character, a whole sexual revolution was consummated. At the beginning of the decade the working-class experience had been incorporated within the novel; rapidly there followed an emphasis on the experience of women. Apart from Lynne Reid Banks (b. 1929) and Nell Dunn (b. 1927), already mentioned, there arrived Edna O'Brien (b. 1936) with *The Country Girls* (1960), *The Lonely Girl* (1962), *Girls in their Married Bliss* (1964) and *August is a Wicked Month* (1965); Penelope Mortimer (b. 1918) with *The Pumpkin Eater* (1962), and Margaret Drabble, with *A Summer Bird-cage* (1963), *The Millstone* (1965) and *The Waterfall* (1969), all related to the role of women in contemporary society. The new wave of feminism, which, in part, was a reaction against the male chauvinist aspects of much of sixties culture, was not yet: the most strongly feminist novel, *The Snow Ball* (1964), came from Bridget Brophy (b. 1929), who had already made her name in the fifties.

Deeper purposes now informed the work of Angus Wilson: *The Old Men at the Zoo* (1961) is a nightmare of the political future (and satire on the Macmillan government); *Late Call*

(1964) reveals the present nightmare if a new town with its new but useless values; while *The Middle Age of Mrs Eliot* is a remarkably warm and sympathetic portrait. The novels of Iris Murdoch, from *A Severed Head* (1961) to *The Sacred and Profane Love Machine* (1974), became ever more complex and contorted, ever more loaded with symbolism, ever deeper in the philosophical puzzles they struggle with. With his novels of the excessive teenage violence of the future, *A Clockwork Orange* (1963) and *The Clockwork Testaments* (1974), and the grumpily surrealistic *Inside Mr Enderby* (1963), Anthony Burgess placed himself on the permanent way to literary esteem. John Fowles also went well outside the traditional novels of social custom with *The Collector* (1963), *The Magus* (1966) and *The French Lieutenant's Woman* (1969), though critics have generally seen him as essentially no more than a middle-brow writer. Martin Amis's *The Rachel Papers* (1973) was reminiscent in some ways of the classic American fifties novel of adolescence, *The Catcher in the Rye* by J. D. Salinger, while some of the humorous formulations were reminiscent of father Kingsley. Socially, the novel marked a kind of culmination of the sixties celebration of youth. *Dead Babies* (1975) − the title embodies the contemptuous phrase which the arrogant, self-indulgent, super-rich characters apply to notions of decency − is a drunken and drugged binge set in the future, quite remarkably anticipating the vicious selfishness which was to become the hallmark of one aspect of the Britain of Mrs Thatcher.

Full middle-brow (at the very least) status was now accorded to the novels (by Brian Aldiss, J. G. Ballard, Ray Bradbury and Arthur C. Clarke) making up the 'new wave' of science fiction, a most important sixties phenomenon. So also to the high-quality spy thrillers of John Le Carré (pseudonym of D. J. M. Cornwell, b. 1931, author of, *inter alia*, *The Spy Who Came in From the Cold* (1963), *Tinker, Tailor, Soldier, Spy* (1974), *The Little Drummer Girl* (1983)), Len Deighton and Dick Francis. The German critic Jans Peter Becker, while noting that British spy and crime writers of the time owed pretty well nothing to American examples, calls Deighton 'the legitimate heir of Chandler and Hammett.'[10]

Changes were taking place in the means whereby books

reached their public. Both the great London commercial circulating libraries and the local twopenny libraries withdrew from business in the early sixties. Two institutions filled the gap. First of all, the public libraries, which up till the Second World War had seen their duties as being basically concerned with the lending of non-fiction works, by the 1964 Libraries and Museums Act, had their position confirmed as the officially recognized centres for making books available; libraries were now, as a number of commentators have remarked, the National Health Service for books. Secondly, the small shops switched over to selling paperbacks.

In the sixties the British were still the greatest library users in the world, with about one-third of the population registered with a public library; but as buyers of books the British ranked well below the Americans and most West Europeans. The absolute number of books produced shot up in the sixties as publishers endeavoured to cash in on affluence by publishing works of history, popular sociology and so on; the number of novels dropped slightly as compared with the fifties. In 1963 2,375 new novels were published, which does not compare very impressively with the 2,153 published in 1937. Sales, in general, were more than they had been in the thirties. To break even, a first novel had to sell about a thousand copies. An average sale of 1,200–1,400 might be expected, but of this 90 per cent went to libraries. British novels, at 60,000 words, tended to be short compared with American. This, according to John Sutherland, author of *Fiction and the Fiction Industry* (1978), was so that dedicated readers could read six novels a fortnight in the half an hour allocated each evening in bed.

Despite innovations elsewhere in Britain, and despite the major experiments taking place on the Continent, the British novel remained fundamentally naturalistic. Margaret Drabble, in 1967, declared: 'I'd rather be at an end of a dying tradition which I admire, than at the beginning of a tradition which I deplore.'

Underground poetry entirely apart, there continued to be movements and groups of poets appealing, in the traditional way, to rather limited audiences. 'The Group' had originally consisted of Cambridge undergraduates, all influenced by the famous Dr F. R. Leavis, and was continued in London in the mid-fifties under the chairmanship of Philip Hobsbaum . Their work came to the attention of a wider audience with the publication of *A Group Anthology* in 1963. Among the poets represented were Philip Hobsbaum (b. 1932), the original founder of the Group; Edward Lucie-Smith (b. 1933), who subsequently took over chairing it; Peter Porter (b. 1929), an Australian; and George MacBeth (b. 1932). In considering what was special about the developments of the sixties, it is instructive to start off with Scotland. The 'Scottish Literary Renaissance' is usually, correctly in my view, seen as having begun in the 1920s; in the post-war years a high critical reputation was enjoyed by Hugh MacDiarmid (1892–1978), Robert Garrioch (b. 1909), Norman MacCaig (b. 1910) and Edwin Morgan (b. 1920), all active figures in a clearly visible Scottish bohemia. What happened in the sixties was that the wider Scottish society (traditionally governed by strongly puritan tenets), or at least parts of it, was brought into a closer alignment with this bohemia while the poets themselves developed a new self-awareness and confidence. Edwin Morgan, in discussing the 1960s, speaks of 'the sort of seriousness or awareness that Scottish poetry has been jolted into (as opposed to certain stereotypes of "entertainment" and "character" which have always been available).'[11] The poet of Orkney, George Mackay Brown (b. 1921), emerged into a more public light, being joined by Alan Jackson and, later, by Alan Bold (b. 1942) who (early works, at least) was a conscious carrier of MacDiarmid's Marxist torch. Morgan records 'poems with monsters – death, alcoholism, war, heroin, the atom.'[12] Most dramatic (in an exact use of that much abused term) was D. M. Black (b. 1941); but Morgan also draws attention to the 'tranquil' poetry of, in particular, Ian Hamilton Finlay (b. 1925), described by Lucie-Smith as 'the most important figure in the British Concrete Poetry Movement.'[13] Analogous developments, involving such poets as Dannie Abse, took place in Wales. Writing in the poetry magazine *Agenda*, the English poet Kathleen Raine stated: 'Much fine verse is being written in Scotland and for a like density of concentration of good poets one would have to go to Wales.'[14]

Of British poetry as a whole in this period it could be said that it was both more ambitious, the limited subject matter and the formalism of the Movement being pushed to the side, and that it involved more people, both as practitioners and as audience. The political edge is very apparent in George MacBeth's 'Funeral-song to America for her Negro dead in Vietnam':

> *. . . I make you the music*
> *of hunger and blood*
> *crying for redress. America, listen. You have raided*
> *the inarticulate one time*
> *too many. The reckoning comes . . .*

Addressing the question of the significance of the sixties, Peter Porter, in 1971, put it this way:

I think the poet has come out from cover a bit more. He no longer apologises for being a poet to all his friends who are something more respectable. To that extent he's emerged. I suppose the poet is no longer such a figure from the higher culture. He's no longer educated necessarily at the best Universities, nor is he necessarily a middle-class figure as he always was . . .

It's now accepted that the poetic calling is open to anyone who, as it were, can get the call.

Porter recognized this as 'an improvement', but could not resist adding a reservation: 'but, mind you, the old principle of exclusiveness kept out a lot of what they might have called "creeps", and now an awful lot of creeps get in, because all you've got to do is set up your plate.'[15] It should be recorded here that the part played by women was a rather constrained one. In the Schmidt and Lindop volume on *British Poetry since 1960* (1972), Margaret Byers styled her contribution 'Cautious Vision: Recent British Poetry by Women': she noted that the majority of women poets confined themselves to the area of middle-class sensibilities, singling out Rosemary Tonks, Fleur Adcock, and Elaine Feinstein as more characteristic of the dynamism of the times.

Most noteworthy among the changing conditions of production and consumption were the practices associated with the 'underground': poetry readings, poetry and jazz, public protest poetry, all gave the audience an importance not usual with traditional 'ivory tower' poetry. The climacteric of 'underground poetry', in the eyes of its anthologist, Michael Horovitz, came at the 1965 International Poetry Incarnation held in the massive Albert Hall, venue for both symphony and pop concerts.[16] Of greater importance for poetry of a less public type, was the proliferation of 'the Little Magazine and the Small Press'.[17] The palm is usually given to Ian Hamilton's *The Revue*, which featured poetry from Scotland and the North of England. Jon Silkin, a poet who in the later sixties was based first in Leeds and then in Newcastle, had founded *Stand* in 1952, but its glory days — supported by an Arts Council subsidy — were those of the sixties and early seventies; *Agenda* I have already mentioned. Harry Chambers was responsible for *Phoenix*, which played its part in widening the geographical circles of poetic involvement when in 1967 it moved with Chambers to Belfast (where, also, it may be noted, Hobsbaum taught for a time): among the local poets *Phoenix* published was Seamus Heaney (b. 1939).

In a way which was again particular to the sixties, foreign influences, primarily American, then German, are evident in a fair amount of British poetry. 'Have I set the tree/askew on your sky,/does your bird hover strangely?'[18] Mathew Mead (b. 1924), in his poem 'Translator to Translated', asked of the East German poet Johannes Nobrowski, whom he translated. Michael Hamburger (b. 1924) and Christopher Middleton (b. 1926) also were energetic translators of modern German poetry; Charles Tomlinson (b. 1927) revealed a whole range of continental and American influences, as did Peter Levi (b. 1931); as with the artist R. J. Kitaj, post-Poundian or 'Black Mountain' poetry was a preoccupation. There was a wider audience for American poetry; probably a small one for German, though the pre-Hitler poet Rainer Maria Rilke enjoyed something of a vogue, the specialist Hogarth Press following *Poems 1906 to 1926* (1957) with *New Poems* (1964) which presented the originals as well as translations. *Modern Poetry in Translation* was instituted in 1963 by Ted Hughes and Daniel Weissbort.

Hughes (b. 1930) exploded (for once the cliché is apt) on the literary scene in 1957 with *Hawk in the Rain*. In his representations of the savagery of life there are parallels with both Golding and Bacon. Throughout the period since he has been the most powerful of British poets; he became Poet Laureate in 1984. Everyone knew of his marriage in 1956 to American 'golden girl' Sylvia Plath (1932–63), whose, 'confessional' poems found an important audience – especially, of course, after her suicide in 1963.

In the world of music – embracing concert hall, radio (in 1964 a daytime Music Programme, was adjoined to the evening Third Programme, the two in 1970 becoming Radio 3, supreme purveyor of classical music), records – non-British works continued overwhelmingly to dominate the market, with the two most notable alterations in taste being a swing towards the symphonies of Mahler at the beginning of the decade, and towards 'early music' (including performance on 'early' instruments) at the end of it.[19] Recording companies, of course, were engaged on a constant search for new products; still the (relative) turning away from the Romantic classics of the later nineteenth century and the search for authenticity in performance can reasonably be linked to the spirit of dissent and innovation apparent in other cultural spheres.

The native giants continued to be Britten and Tippett, the significant development being that in the early sixties the latter began to achieve the recognition which had previously eluded him, while around 1970 there was a positive upsurge of enthusiasm. Mainly, Tippett's political commitment and his sheer energy and inventiveness in incorporating a massive range of influences in his powerful music, caught the predilections of a changing audience; partly he was helped (as certainly younger composers were helped) by sponsorship of modern (as well as early) music by William Glock, the BBC's Controller of Music (1959–72). Tippett's opera *The Knot Garden* (1966–9), set in a country house and garden, and focusing on the resolution of amorous difficulties through play-acting, includes jazz and blues, references to Mozart's *Cosi fan tutte*, and combines 'the rapid cross-cutting of King Priam with the exuberant flow of *The Midsummer Marriage*'.[20] Great acclaim greeted the Third Symphony (1970), which included a soprano blues in the finale; *The Ice Break* (1973–6), an opera in which Tippett's political commitments are manifest in his treatment of conflicts between races, generations and parties; the Fourth Symphony (1976–7), and *The Mask of Time* (1977–82), an oratorio 'which in its multifarious literary and musical borrowings, and in its conviction, is Tippett's summa'.[21]

Benjamin Britten died in 1976. He had continued to write operas specifically for the English Opera Group, always with particular singers in mind (a more important 'condition of production' than it may seem). *A Midsummer Night's Dream* (1960) contrives an emphasis that is not explicit in Shakespeare, symbolizing sleep and dreams as the familiar gateway to a blessed realm of fantasy that is otherwise accessible only through enchantment.[22] *Owen Wingrave* (1970) was conceived for television (another important 'condition of production'), and *Death in Venice* (1973), produced with sets by John Piper, was one of the great cultural events of the age. Japanese influences are strong in *Curlew River* (1964), the first of three 'parables for church performance'. His last important work was the *Third String Quartet* (1975), which may be seen as bringing resolution to the dialectic between the traditional and the modern in musical language.

Younger radicals looked in a firmly modern direction, influenced by the continuing innovations abroad of Karlheinz Stockhausen and Olivier Messiaen, and of Pierre Boulez, who conducted the BBC Symphony Orchestra in the early sixties. The London Sinfonietta was an important force in the playing of contemporary music. In all this parallels with, say, the 'New Generation' sculptors are very clear, though for once, the musical avant-garde actually appeared a decade earlier, in, in fact, mid-fifties Manchester, where Harrison Birtwhistle, Peter Maxwell Davies and Alexander Goehr (son of a German refugee) were all pupils at the Royal Manchester College of Music. These three, in common with other modernists such as Richard Rodney Bennett and Nicholas Maw, all had periods of study in continental Europe; Peter Racine Fricker and Iain Hamilton (whose operas *The Catiline Conspiracy* (1974), and *The Royal Hunt of the Sun* (1977), were performed, respectively, by Scottish Opera and the English National Opera), both moved, early in the sixties, to permanent jobs in the United States: all of which was entirely in keeping with the cosmopolitanism and ferment of cultural exchange of this new era in the arts.

So also was the rise and rise of photography. If British intellectuals before the sixties had generally been scornful of film as a cultural form they had scarcely realized that photography had any pretensions to that status at all. Some commentators did, and do, it is true, make much of the British documentary movement of the thirties, associated with the film-maker John Grierson, though probably finding its most impressive expression in the pages of *Picture Post*, which set out to 'document' social conditions and ordinary lifestyles, often (in my view) in a manner which was both artificial and patronising. The photographer's photographer from the thirties onwards was Bill Brandt, who certainly did produce magnificent visual documents of British life (many of which I have most gratefully used myself). The leading 'arty' photographer was Cecil Beaton, very much a minority taste. But *the* medium for recording and fostering certain aspects of sixties culture was, as the film *Blow Up* recognized, photography. It was a development very closely associated with the rise of a new kind of professional model, personified by Jean Shrimpton and Twiggy ('mannequins' previously had generally been aristocratic ladies), and the emphasis on 'the beautiful people' and the swinging lifestyle. A highly dramatic, even flashy, mode was called for. Cameras were to art and advertising what washing machines were to domestic life: they fitted well into the international (the Germans were the great innovators) and, fairly, classless world of gadgetry. Upper-class figures Anthony Armstrong-Jones and Patrick Lichfield led the way, quickly joined by three upwardly mobile products of the London working class – David Bailey, Terrence Donovan and Brian Duffy. There were, of course, some brilliant (and brave) news photographers of whom the doyen was Don McCullin, also a product of working-class London.

But if photography was often the lackey to flash commercialism, it could also be the servant of art – as David Hockney and Gilbert and George were to show. Architecture, servant of some of the noblest of post-war idealism, became in the sixties the cruel master of the destinies of masses of defenceless people. In this unhappy realm of public housing, the decade began with a warning and ended with a disaster. In 1961 the Ministry of Housing and Local Government report *Homes for Today and Tomorrow* (the Sir Parker Morris report) called for local authorities and architects to heed the real needs of real people; but the plea was largely ignored, and since whatever the deep-seated weaknesses in the British economy, the sixties were a time of economic expansion and 're-development', the errors of the fifties were multiplied. High-rise accommodation needs to be linked to certain amenities, such as functioning lifts and proper security, as it is when supplied privately to the wealthier classes. When excessive economies are applied in conjunction with daft theories about working-class gregariousness and housing as public monument, the results can only be disastrous. In his autobiography (published in 1967) Walter Greenwood, author of the great working-class novel of the 1930s, *Love on the Dole*, spoke enthusiastically about what was happening to the former slum area in Lancashire where he was brought up:

Bulldozers are at their work of destruction here ... Over three decades have passed since I stood on the threshold of what proved to be for me a wonderful year, decades that have witnessed another world war, the voluntary liquidation of the Empire and the establishment of a social revolution of which this demolition is but a local aspect.

The 're-development' of central Newcastle carried out by T. Dan Smith and his colleagues received the praises of the left-wing intellectual journal the *New Statesman*. When the Kirby housing estate near Liverpool — later to become a paradigm of dereliction and vandalism — was opened, Barbara Castle, left-wing member of the Labour government, told the local Labour party: 'This is your chance to build a new Jerusalem.' In fact the bulldozers lauded by Walter Greenwood were engaged on a destructive foray against close-knit older communities for the poor trade-off of disruptive urban motor-ways and ugly, unloved high-rise housing (though there were successful estates, such as Ralph Erskine's carefully integrated Byker development in Newcastle). In 1968 a gas explosion brought the collapse of Roman Point, a systems-built tower block in East London. Much else collapsed as well; and architects and planners must be given credit for the fact that by the time the seventies had begun they were obviously aware that they had an architectural and planning crisis on their hands. A new emphasis on conservation and a halt to the building of high-rise public housing were announced (second-generation new towns, such as Milton Keynes, building throughout the seventies and eighties, stuck to low-rise) though low-cost housing estates of dubious popularity would go on being built, and thousands of people would continue for many years to be marooned in flats hundreds of feet above the ground.

But the cultural ferment of the 1960s also called for the building and extending of universities, and the building of theatres; and some of the attempts at building integrated communities for living in were quite successful. Stylistically, one could make a rough distinction between the monumental terrace style of Sir Denys Lasdun, as seen in the university of East Anglia and the National Theatre, and also in Patrick Hodgkinson's Brunswick Centre in Bloomsbury, and the gentler more flexible style of, say, Sir Basil Spence with his Sussex University, strongly influenced by Le Corbusier's Jaoul houses in Paris and discreetly blending echoes of a Roman coliseum into a magnificent landscape. There had, of course, to be something going on in Liverpool, and that was the building, between 1960 and 1967, of Frederick Gibberd's Roman Catholic cathedral: this is a striking building, certainly making as dramatic a break from the traditions of Christian architecture as did Spence's Coventry cathedral, but, built to a restricted budget, it has been criticised for its lack of coherence. The impressive 'crown of thorns' which surmounts the circular building became known locally as 'a cooling tower' – the Mersey funnel'.[23] The first custom-built open stage theatre was that for the Chichester Festival, completed in 1961 by the firm of Powell and Moya. After a chequered and sometimes murky history the Nottingham

Playhouse project came to a successful conclusion in the same year with an effective building by Peter Moro and Partners.

Less noted at the time than they were subsequently, were a number of buildings designed by Scottish-born, Liverpool-educated James Stirling, within the partnership he had formed with James Gowan: the engineering building at Leicester university (completed 1964), the Cambridge university history faculty (finished 1968), and the student residences at Oxford, the Florey Building (1966--71) which Jencks sees as a summation of Stirling's previous work:

It has the sharp visual contrast of Leicester, the shimmering prismatic glass versus bright red tile. It has the sloping section and circulation discipline of Cambridge, the exposed exhaust stacks and elevator towers of all his projects and that uncanny fragmented geometry − here five eighths of an octagon which is stretched round the public rooms and given a strong sense of enclosure. The forms, while not directly derivative, remind one more of those which clothed the heroic functions of post-revolutionary Russia, than they connote musings of Oxford undergraduate life.[24]

That, for some, of course, was the trouble.

In part I, it was easy for me to allocate a separate chapter or section to each art form, in standard text book fashion. But the sixties was an age for abandoning standard text books, one in which different cultural practices meshed and interrelated with each other. 'The snobbery which used to exist' certainly did not totally disappear, and could very readily revive again. Neither a working-class culture, nor anything that could sensibly be called 'an alternative culture' triumphed. Cultural change is cumulative not dialectical. Cultures, like classes, adapt, incorporate new elements, respond to challenges. The changes of the sixties continued in the seventies and still profoundly affect cultural life today.

Notes

1 Elizabeth Nelson, *British Counter-Culture, 1966–1973* (1989); *Thanks for Coming* (1984) by Jim Haynes is the autobiography of one of the more endearing figures of the 'counter-culture', who recognizes the naive optimism of his 'revolutionary' hopes.

2 Quoted in Nelson, *British Counter-Culture*, p. 98.

3 Edward Lucie-Smith (ed.), *British Poetry since 1945* (1985), p. 335.

4 W. E. Parkinson, 'Poetry in the North East', in Michael Schmidt and Grevel Lindop (eds), *British Poetry since 1960* (1972), pp. 116–21.

5 Ronald Hayman, *The Set-Up: An Anatomy of English Theatre Today* (1973), pp. 307–9.

6 Ibid., p. 116.

7 Ibid., pp. 229–301.

8 Ibid., p. 116.

9 In October 1971 a spot-check at Wyndham's revealed that 48.1 per cent of tickets sold went to foreign tourists (ibid., p. 143).

10 In C. W. E. Bigsby (ed.), *Superculture: American Popular Culture and Europe* (1975), pp. 157–8.

11 Edwin Morgan, 'Scottish Poetry in the 1960s', in Michael Schmidt and Grevel Lindop (eds), *British Poetry since 1960* (1972).

12 Ibid.

13 Lucie-Smith, *British Poetry*, p. 310.

14 Quoted by Glyn Jones, in 'Second Flowering: Poetry in Wales', in Schmidt and Lindop, *British Poetry*, p. 130.

15 Quoted in Schmidt and Lindop, *British Poetry*, p. 212.

16 Michael Horovitz, *Children of Albion: Poetry of the 'Underground'* (1969), p. 337.

17 The title of the essay by Harry Chambers in Schmidt and Lindop, *British Poetry*.

18 Lucie-Smith, *British Poetry*, p. 215.

19 Paul Griffiths 'Music', in *The Cambridge Guide to the Arts in Britain: Since the Second World War* (ed. Boris Ford, 1988), p. 50.

20 Ibid., p. 63.

21 Ibid., p. 63.

22 Peter Evans, *The Music of Benjamin Britten* (1979), p. 237.

23 Charles Jencks, *Modern Movements in Architecture*, (1973), p. 24.

24 Ibid., p. 269.

Part III

The Return of Gradgrind: 1977–1990

11 The End of Consensus

In very many respects the new lifestyles and modes of behaviour which came fully into being in the 1960s continued throughout the seventies and the eighties. However, nothing can be more certain than that the conditions of cultural production and consumption at the end of the eighties were utterly different from what they had been in the early seventies. No single phrase can be all-explaining, let alone painstakingly accurate, yet the hackneyed one I have put at the head of this chapter really does come as near to fitting the bill as any phrase could. Beneath 'the end of consensus', which is a political and social phenomenon, lay, of course, critical economic developments. The economy had been performing inadequately in comparison with international competitors since the early fifties, with un-redeemed structural weaknesses going back to the forties. However, as long as the great international boom, touched off in the first instance by the breaking out of all the demand suppressed during the war years, lasted, Britain could coast along with living standards steadily rising. In 1973 the oil-producing nations doubled oil prices, throwing the world into recession. Britain (though, ironically, just becoming an oil-producing nation herself), having, in particular, consistently failed to channel investment into productive industry, was ill-fitted to meet the new challenge. By the middle of the decade inflation had reached 23 per cent. Thereafter, partly through restrictions on credit and demand, partly through the application of a very rigid incomes policy, the rate was steadily brought down. High inflation always causes grievance and resentment for certain groups; a rigid incomes policy always causes suffering and bitterness for other social groups. Meantime, in August 1975 unemployment figures passed the two million mark, effectively signalling the end of the postwar full employment economy, a crucial buttress of consensus. Unemployment went on rising until 1977, then was actually reduced slightly in 1978 and 1979.

The Labour government which was in office from 1974 to 1979 set out to implement its 'Social Contract' whose essence was that in recognition of the sacrifice in wage increases there would be enhanced welfare benefits: the ultimate in 'consensus', but also consensus's last fling. Benefits went to the low-paid and the unfortunate; skilled workers really preferred wage increases. In any case, as the British Exchequer ran out of funds, the Chancellor, Denis Healey, had to go begging to the International Monetary Fund. In return for loans, this body insisted on severe conditions. Substantial public expenditure cuts were imposed in 1976, the year in which, some commentators say, monetarism began: the chisels were out for another buttress of consensus, high government spending on social welfare and also (our particular concern) on culture.

Inside the Labour party there had always been fundamentalist left-wing opposition to the consensus policies of Labour governments in office; the theory usually put forward in the sixties was that the left-wingers should split off and form a minority fundamentalist party of their own. Between the later seventies and the early eighties the balance of forces within the Labour movement changed drastically. Low-paid workers (including many women workers), organized through the National Union of Public Employees (NUPE), showed a new self-consciousness, and NUPE itself went through an astonishing growth in the late seventies. At the same time, as the ideas of post-structuralism and linguistic materialism spread in intellectual circles, there was a great resurgence of various brands of Marxism throughout the party. Had the Labour party won the 1979 general election these developments might have been contained; as it was, the victory by the Conservatives under Margaret Thatcher gave them an enormous stimulus.

As the Labour party moved left, the Conservative party

moved right. The new government had a secure majority of 43 in parliament and thus could, if it wished, push through the radical right policies espoused by Thatcher and her closest associates: and it did so wish. But with respect to the popular suffrage, only 43.9 per cent of those voting had voted Conservative, while 36.9 had still voted Labour. The pushing through of radical measures, to which less than 50 per cent of the population had given support, could not but increase social divisions. Again, however, we cannot ignore the world economic situation. The fact is that not long after the Thatcher ministry took office the international trade recession worsened sharply. In this context the government's determination to adhere strictly to the principles of monetarism and ruthlessly to curtail public spending had very serious repercussions. Unemployment in 1979 had eased to 5.7 per cent. In 1980−1 it took off astronomically and by the end of 1982 had more than doubled, with a rate of 13.4 per cent, and the highest ever number of people out of work, 3,190,621. De-industrialization was striking with a vengeance. A bitter and violent strike in the steel industry in 1980 failed to stop closures and job losses (the government, however, for the time being avoided any confrontation with the miners). The West Midlands joined with Scotland, the North and Wales as an area in which manufacturing industry was drastically shrinking, the queues for unemployment benefit lengthening. Yet the rate of inflation, down to 9.3 per cent in 1978−9, almost doubled in 1979−80 to 18.4 per cent, and was running at 13.0 per cent in 1980−1, though down to 8.6 per cent in 1981−2. Government spending controls meant that there was a significant erosion in the spending power of welfare benefits. Over the period 1979 to 1983 manufacturing production declined by more than 15 per cent. As militant left-wing elements became stronger and stronger on some major local authorities, such as the Greater London Council and the Merseyside Metropolitan Council, the scene was set for as sharp a series of confrontations as had ever been seen between local and central government.

Yet, in the early months of 1982 it was still not possible to say that consensus had irreversibly broken down. Supporters of consensual politics within the Conservative party seemed to be in a strong position as Mrs Thatcher's popularity slumped. Supporters of centrist politics within the Labour party had formed the Social Democratic Party: predictions were that in any future general election votes would be shared fairly evenly between this new party, Labour and the Conservatives. However, the Falklands war (2 April-14 June, 1982) restored Mrs Thatcher's fortunes, and she went on to win the election of June 1983, though with fewer votes than she had gained in 1979. Thatcherism could now be released in full flood. What this entailed was:

1   The accelerated run-down of Britain's industrial base (while in the later eighties there was a marked upturn in the iron and steel industry, levels still scarcely reached those of the late seventies).

2   An emphasis on the virtues of unrestricted private enterprise responding simply to the demands of the market. After 1983 there was a considerable expansion in the service trades of various sorts – financial services, legal services, retailing of all kinds.

3   As a result mainly of these two developments, the south of the country became quite prosperous, thus marking it off sharply from a much less prosperous north.

4   However, the two biggest social consequences, unemployment and homelessness, touched southern areas as well as northern ones.

5   A switch away from community-based values to those based on individual enterprise and on the market. With respect to our subject this had two main implications: (a) the arts would need to look to private sponsorship rather than state patronage; (b) the status of art would be determined more by popularity than by the qualities of (as I call it) 'serious art'.

Recession and high unemployment greatly reduced the powers of trade unions: these economic developments were probably more important than the various employment acts passed by the Thatcher government to limit the rights and privileges of unions. But if strike action was at a discount, the bitterness and division within British society in the eighties was most characteristically expressed in horrific new levels of urban rioting, beginning in Brixton in south London in April 1981, then emerging in the summer in Toxteth, central Liverpool, Moss Side, Manchester, Bristol, Leicester, and several areas in London. But there were also violent confrontations between special police groups and workers taking industrial action. First there was the confrontation towards the end of 1983 at the Stockport plant of provincial newspaper proprietor, and enthusiastic proponent of the new information technology, Eddie Shah, then there was the year-long miners' strike of 1984−5. In the autumn of 1985 there was more rioting, first in Handsworth in Birmingham, then Brixton, then Toxteth, then Tottenham in north east London. In 1986 clashes took place between police and workers refusing to accept conditions of employment at the new News International plant at Wapping in London's East End. Urban deprivation and racial discrimination, new employer-worker relations and changing technology— there were the roots of urban and industrial confrontation respectively.

But violence was now appearing everywhere and often apparently quite randomly. Addressing a conference in Surrey on alcohol-related crime in January 1989, the local Chief Constable declared that 'stronger family and church ties, and teachers able to mete out physical punishment, were needed to quell "rising violence"'. Left-wing commentators, naturally, put the blame on high unemployment, despair and aimlessness among the country's youth, the fostering of aggressive economic selfishness, and the policies of polarization and confrontation pursued by the Thatcher government. The traditional police view was not altogether wrong. What was happening was that the old reference points by which individuals and groups measured their behaviour, and by which their behaviour was constrained, had drastically changed. Society had been more unified under policies which deliberately sought to avoid unemployment and to sustain social benefits, policies which recognized the place of trade unions in society, and policies which upheld tolerance and civilized behaviour as important values. Football hooligans at home saw themselves as fighting for their own particular community; football hooligans abroad, ironically, saw themselves as demonstrating British might. All this was, however distortedly, in keeping with the values of the aggressive market place and the Falklands war. There were no longer national communal values to which all but the most desperate and alienated subscribed. Loyalty was now to the individual peer group. And for many gangs of young people the highest values attached to demonstrations of contempt for citizens and families bent on enjoying the modest rewards of a quiet and industrious life. As acquisitiveness was now being publicly sanctioned, why not brutally attack those blessed with goods that one did not have oneself? Structural trends were breaking up old national loyalties and communal networks: those in authority were hastening the trends, and putting nothing appropriate in the place of the loyalties and networks. Despite apparent quiescence, and some signs of economic upturn, Britain at the beginning of the nineties was still, as never since 1945, a country of confrontation (as poll tax demonstrations showed) and separate sub-cultures.

Particularly relevant to our concerns are feminist culture and homosexual culture (here, unusually in this book, I am using the word 'culture' in the wider sense). The consensus idea behind the reforms of the sixties had been that both women and male homosexuals should be integrated fully into mainstream society. In fact, for a variety of reasons, including the continuing prejudices of sections of the press and public, the mobilization for left-wing political purposes of minority groups and gay liberation ideology (emanating in particular from America), gay culture became very much a separate cultural phenomenon.

A third election victory by the Conservatives under Margaret Thatcher in 1987 might seem to suggest that Thatcherite values now had a firm grip on the country. There can be no doubt that in certain areas of intellectual and artistic endeavour there was a strong conservative tide, a rejection of the experimentation of the sixties and early seventies. In the visual and plastic arts there was indeed something of a return to both figurism and traditional materials; direct political statement was at a discount. At the same time, much art and literature was clearly critical of the kind of selfish, divided society, where money is god, associated with Thatcherism. Nor would it be accurate to contrast a New Piety of the eighties with the permissiveness of the sixties: Gilbert and George are the artists most usually associated with Thatcherism, but in their use of four-letter words and photographs of the male member their works are more explicit than any art of the sixties. It is not in fact always easy to distinguish between the crude populism of the radical right ideology of the eighties and the pop trends of the sixties. And, flatly counter to radical right ideas, there was a stronger than ever espousal in some quarters of the ideas of post-structuralism and linguistic materialism. In this connection an important event in 1976 (and indeed one of my subsidiary reasons for placing the starting point of part three in the seventies) was the publication of *Notes for a New Culture: An Essay on Modernism* by Peter Åckroyd. Ackroyd's central purpose was 'to counter the general malaise of English literature and literary studies', by drawing attention to 'the emergence of LANGUAGE as the content of literature and as the form of knowledge'.[1] Some commentators lumped together all of these developments – jokey populism, 'heritage architecture', post-structuralism, linguistic materialism – under the modish label, 'post-modernism',[2] a word which, in fact, is perhaps better applied to certain intellectual theories than to any alleged movement in the arts.

In Scotland, where the electorate was consistently anti-Thatcher and where the Conservatives looked in some danger of being entirely wiped out, there was, by the early eighties, a great surge in the sense of a separate Scottish identity. While many of the same heritage-style market-orientated developments seemed to be taking place in the major Scottish cities, there was a strong feeling that, being essentially sponsored and directed by the local authorities, these were in keeping with a distinctive Scottish sense of community. More perhaps than ever before, we need in cultural matters to look out for a separate Scottishness. At the same time, though, and particularly when looking at the English part of the kingdom, we must recognize that an important part of the whole Thatcherite spirit was a welcoming into Britain of all things thought to pertain to American culture. In fact, though the sixties are the great age of opening up to cosmopolitan influences, the eighties is the era of internationalization. From the time of the ratification of Britain's membership of the European Common Market in 1975 contacts with the European continent multiplied rapidly; and Japanese influences, usually in the form of a kind of recycled Americanization, joined with the directly American ones. Information technology was, both in method and subject matter, a potent agent of internationalization.

Class continues to be a critical factor in cultural production and consumption. The key developments in the years of privatization were an acceleration in the breaking up of the rigid frontiers of the working class (a process long talked about, but less readily perceivable as an actual reality), and more abrupt openings to positions of power and influence for people who had not taken the trouble to absorb the traditional upper-class lifestyle. The much-talked of 'yuppy', though over-publicized, did have corporeal existence. In this era of buying and selling (in *information* services, shares, development land, and goods of all kinds) there were large incomes and commissions to be earned in finance, accountancy, law, in agencies and consultancies of all kinds, as well as in commerce. That, combined with vigorous propaganda on behalf of the notion that success was far more important than social origins (not everyone believed the propaganda – including some of the propagandist), was the basis for the yuppy phenomenon. Exact statistics are lacking, but impressionistic evidence indicates that working-class and lower-middle-class forms of speech, and provincial accents, were being heard as never before in the world of finance and the commercially oriented professions (I have already attributed the accent breakthrough to the sixties, but in the areas I am now speaking of upper-class accents, whether natural or assumed, would have been expected throughout the seventies). Change was most obvious in the Conservative party itself, as each successive Conservative victories brought into Parliament more successful entrepreneurs, consultants etc. who had not been beneficiaries of the traditional upper-class education, while upholders of traditional upper-class culture were (up to a point) in retreat.

For class structure as a whole, and the nature of the working class in particular, we have the important empirical work by Marshall, Newby, Rose and Vogler,[3] who came up with the figures of 58 per cent of the population working-class and 42 per cent middle-class. As always happens, the raw survey material underestimates the continuing existence of an upper class (the upper class tend to be concentrated in particular areas, and there is in any case a polite convention that one does not actually call oneself upper class), giving the following responses:

Upper	0.2 per cent
Upper middle	3.0 per cent
Middle	23.7 per cent
Lower middle	11.8 per cent
Upper working	11.1 per cent
Working	37.6 per cent
Lower working	4.2 per cent
(Refused)	2.8 per cent
(Don't know)	5.6 per cent

(*Source*: Marshall et al., *Social Class in Modern Britain*, p. 114)

These figures tell us of a very clear sense that classes still exist. The exact allocation to class is, of course, personal and subjective, but the broad figures do coincide remarkably well with the hard statistical information which exists on different types of occupation, manual and non-manual. Usually there is a slight tendency for a few of those who, by other economic and social criteria, definitely are working-class to allocate themselves to the middle class. Thus, it would probably not be far wrong if we took the 58 per cent figure as an accurate one for the size of the working class in the mid 1980s, and if we compare this with the 69.8 per cent figure produced by Richard Scase in 1972,[4] we would have a good measure of social change in the intervening period. Perhaps 39 per cent would be a roughly appropriate figure for the middle class (to be compared with 19.3 per cent in 1972), leaving about 3 per cent as the figure for the upper class. Marshall, Newby, Rose and Vogler demonstrate conclusively that, as I have always myself insisted, there is a very high sense of class awareness in this reduced working class, though little class consciousness in the

Marxist sense. The authors particularly point to the inequalities with regard to mobility, earnings etc., suffered by women. And, of course, they recognize the salience of race, the disadvantages and the political significance (a strong likelihood of voting Labour) of being non-white. The continuing relevance of class was shown up very starkly in such development areas as the London Docklands. The very high investment of public funds was benefiting the new middle-class and upper-class residents, while long established working-class families were being squeezed out. Was there, therefore, open conflict between the classes? The middle 1980s were marked by one unprecedentedly violent and prolonged industrial dispute, by horrendous urban riots, by terrorism, and by much sporadic strife, which continued into the later eighties when a kind of quiescence seemed to settle over the arena in which capital meets labour. But overall, for all the very real evidence of confrontation in many different areas, Britain was not obviously any more riven by class conflict than it had ever been.

In many of their basic beliefs – in the welfare state, in community services etc. – the British remained remarkably unchanged for all the impact of Thatcherism. The relationship between political shifts and popular attitudes is not a simple one. Nor is it easy to work out the exact relationships between politics, declining government patronage, and cultural trends and achievements. While starving the arts was certainly no recipe for a cultural efflorescence, it was not automatically true that government stinginess would mean death to the arts. The new approaches were encapsulated in the slim but glossy prospectus published by the Arts Council in 1985 entitled *A Great British Success Story*, which spoke quite openly of the 'arts industry', seen as embracing both high and popular culture and all structures and activities relating thereto:

It is the Edinburgh International Festival with its ever expanding Fringe, and the sights and sounds of Carnival filling the streets of Notting Hill ... It is Space-time Systems' Box Office computer system (BOCS) developed in British theatres, and the world-wide consultancy service of Theatre Projects promoting British technical achievements in sound, lighting and solid state engineering.[5]

The nation benefits from investing in the arts, it is explained, because 'most of the money is quickly recouped in taxes'; the arts increase employment at low cost (thus incidentally producing savings in welfare payments); the arts help the regeneration of depressed inner cities; the arts vitalise the wider entertainment industry; the arts raise the nation's prestige; the arts are a substantial tourist attraction and foreign currency earner; and (last, but conceivably not least) the arts give great pleasure to millions of people. Throughout, the document stresses the interrelationship between the growth of the arts and growth of leisure in contemporary society. It concludes with a word on 'productivity and efficiency': 'our product offers excellent value. On average our companies earn around 45 per cent of turn-over, a much higher figure than our rivals in Germany and France . . .[6]

The Arts Council was no longer operating autonomously as it had throughout the years of consensus; it had become an instrument of government policy. Another autonomous source of public money dried up when the Thatcher government abolished the GLC and the Metropolitan counties, which had between them been responsible for arts subsidies of more than £300,000 annually. Everything now had its market value. The Victoria and Albert Museum capitulated most gleefully, introducing admission charges, commissioning Saatchi and Saatchi to produce the crass advertisement 'an ace Caff with quite a nice museum attached', and, in the name of efficient management, carrying through a disastrous series of redundancies among its expert curators. It would be absurd to pretend that there was anything strikingly new about the intertwining of commercialism and the arts. It would be absurd also to deny that the prizes, the sponsorships, the publicity, the hard sells helped to increase awareness of the arts and to further break down 'the snobbery that used to exist'. And it would be myopic to ignore the way in which public galleries were becoming more 'user-friendly'. Under Nicholas Serota, the Tate, in 1990, introduced a new, educationally effective, reorganization of the galleries: the new fuller captions to works of art varied from leftist propaganda (in certain specialist exhibitions), to the helpfully informative (National Gallery and Tate), to the pathetically ignorant (a V&A caption refers to pre-James I 'British' monarchs, when, of course, these were merely English monarchs). But undoubtedly the balance was tipping away from the disinterested funding which had existed throughout the years of consensus: *Observer* art critic William Feaver identified a 'deep, mutually acquistive, involvement of collector-dealer-hyper-artist'.[7]

That whatever people might say about Thatcherite 'morality' and the 'new piety' the new departures of the sixties could not suddenly be blocked was apparent, to choose but one example, in continuing developments in British film censorship. Early in 1989 the British Board of Film Classification (as it was now called) proposed that between the 15 category (suitable for showing to those over fifteen) and the PG category (parental guidance required) there should be a new 12 category. As reported in the *Independent* on 27 January 1989, James Ferman, director of the Board, stated:

Crocodile Dundee is the best example of all. We had to give that a 15 on the single word 'fucking'. It's lunatic that 12, 13 and 14-year-olds should be stopped seeing such an otherwise suitable film because of one word that they probably hear every day. ...

The Board has recently stopped giving films a PG certificate which include 'shitting' and 'arse-hole' but which are unobjectionable in other ways. However, it feels that putting such movies into the 15 class is unduly restrictive.

In 1984, because of (justified) concern about 'video nasties', the Board was given the separate function of classifying video films. British outrage over the Salman Rushdie affair (see chapter 14) was perhaps somewhat blunted when the Board refused a classification to Nigel Wingrove's short video film *Visions of Ecstasy* on the grounds that it would be liable to prosecution under laws still protecting the Christian religion against blasphemy.

Notes

1 Peter Ackroyd, *Notes for a New Culture: An Essay on Modernism* (1976), Introduction.
2 See David Harvey, *The Condition of Postmodernity: an Enquiry into the Origins of Cultural Change* (1989), esp. p. 42.
3 Gordon Marshall, Howard Newby, David Rose and Carolyn Vogler, *Social Class in Modern Britain* (1988).
4 Richard Scase, 'English and Swedish Concepts of Class', in F. Parkin (ed.), *The Social Analysis of Class Structure* (1974), pp. 149–77.
5 Arts Council, *A Great British Success Story* (1985).
6 Ibid.
7 *Observer*, 24 December 1989.

12 Chariots on Fire

Chronically under-capitalized and confused in its aims, the British film industry continued to alternate between 'revivals' and crises.[1] Whereas from the forties to the sixties the industry had averaged well over 100 films a year, by the middle eighties the figure was down to fifty. No British film made it into the top ten British box office successes of the 1980s: biggest money-spinner of all was the Australian-originated, *Crocodile Dundee*; otherwise, American products dominated, usually, apart from the slightly feminist drama *Fatal Attraction* (1987, directed by Adriane Lyne), fantasy films with child-appeal, of the type developed by Steven Spielberg.[2] Nevertheless, British films continued to have a reputation for combining a distinctive character with commercial appeal in America, and one or two films were stylistically as innovative as anything being produced anywhere else in the world. In the same year, 1976, that EMI took over British Lion, a Canadian merchant banker founded Goldcrest to tap the 'strong market demand for good quality feature films for adult and family entertainment which do not depend on explicit sex or violence for their audience appeal'.[3] Within two years Handmade Films (financed mainly by ex-Beatle George Harrison) had been established, specifically in the first instance to make a further Monty Python film, *Life of Brian* (1979), which in its apparent echoes of the life of Jesus was a touch too blasphemous for the film moguls. It was another couple of years before critics were confidently speaking of a British film renaissance, but meantime there had appeared *Midnight Express* (1978, directed by Alan Parker, brilliant individualist, subsequently highly successful in Hollywood), the true and horrific story of an American student jailed in Turkey (David Puttnam, a leading figure at Goldcrest, was one of the two producers), *Yanks* (1979), set in the wartime Lancashire of 1942, and *The Elephant Man* (1980, an EMI—Warner film, directed by David Lynch, telling the harrowing story of a nineteenth-century fairground freak). Up there in the world of the multi-nationals, the British company Thorne Electric took over EMI in 1979.

The up-and-down history of the British film industry demonstrates both strategic failure in defining objectives and matching them to resources, and the continuing existence of both a pool of basic skills and of individuals possessed of genuine creative talent. I have already explained how circumstances came together in the late fifties to create a fertile interaction between theatre and novels (often provincial) and film-making. The sources of change at the beginning of the eighties were slightly different. Although there had been fruitful contacts, received opinion had long held that film and television were deadly rivals. Rapid advances in information technology made it clear to younger and brighter spirits that the whole film—television—video nexus must be treated as providing one integrated market place. Into this market came talent from advertising, generally distinguished in Britain for high technical quality and creative 'attack' (David Puttnam as producer and Hugh Hudson as director are outstanding examples), from TV docudrama (Rowland Joffe is a good example), from the subsidized sectors of the media, now very much on their metal in a time of cuts (Mike Radford and Peter Greenaway had both worked for the Central Office of Information, while the former had also worked for TV, and the latter for subsidized art films), and from the theatre, where sixties drive and innovation had been most thoroughly sustained (Richard Eyre is a good example). The Union Jack label still had considerable appeal in the United States (because of diversification within the American market, it was possible now to aim at specialist American 'art houses' rather than the old mass market): what the film-makers had to do was to put together a package which an American distributor would be prepared to buy in advance. However, there were still also the possibilities of subsidy by the National Film Finance Corporation or even sponsorship through the British Film Institute (both curtailed in the Films Act of 1985 which sought to make the British film industry stands on its own feet in the unmediated market place). But the new and characteristic development came after the establishment of the second commercial television channel, Channel Four, in November 1982. From the start Channel Four directed funds into film-making with the idea that such films would first have theatrical exhibition, then be presented on their own 'Film on Four'.

In every year from 1981 to 1985 inclusive, the British industry produced four or five films which, whether one liked them or not, certainly commanded attention. Chronologically (it was released in January 1981) the first was *The Long Good Friday*, arguably the best British film since *The Third Man* (certainly the music by Francis Monkman matched that of Anton Karas). Independent producer Barry Hanson (he set up his own Calendar films) commissioned the original screenplay in 1977 from socialist writer Barrie Keeffe. Financing came from Lord Grade's Associated Communications Corporation. Directed by John Mackenzie and starring Bob Hoskins and Helen Mirren, *The Long Good Friday* was shot on location in London's docklands in the summer of 1979. The gangster boss of 'The Corporation' (Hoskins) is a Thatcherite gone mad. Brilliantly cut and highly exciting, utterly uninhibited in language (a product, remember, of the years 1977–80), the film captures the moment when collapsing consensus is being replaced by the bombastic claims of 'enterprise culture'; it suggests that Britain is a banana republic, the IRA invincible. ACC decided there would be no profit in general release and decided to go straight for television presentation, in heavily cut form. There was outcry from the film-makers, the actors and certain film critics: James Ferman let it be known that the film could be released without a single cut; Handmade Films put up the cash. They got their investment back within weeks.

Attention, however, is always usually focused on *Chariots of Fire*, released in March 1981 and winning its Oscar for best picture at Hollywood in March 1982. Also released in 1981 were *Tess*, a French co-production, backed by Columbia, and directed by the Polish-American Roman Polanski, and the fetchingly eccentric *Gregory's Girl*, co-produced by Scottish Television and scripted and directed by the gifted and original Scot, Bill Forsythe.

The points I have been endeavouring to make can be most economically pointed up if I now simply list the most important films of the following four years, drawing attention to their most relevant features. From 1982: *Britannia Hospital* (directed by Lindsay Anderson, a satire on the royal celebrations of the day, bringing in the motif of terrorism); *Moonlighting* (made for Channel Four, directed by Jerzy Skolimowski; an off-beat tale, at a time when Poland was hitting the headlines, about a group of Poles desperately earning money by renovating a London house); *The Draughtsman's Contract* (a highly stylized and non-naturalistic fable about power, set in the seventeenth century, made by the BFI and Channel Four, and scripted and directed by Peter Greenaway); *Gandhi* (produced and directed by Richard Attenborough, it seemed to confirm the genuineness of the British renaissance by winning six Oscars, the most ever won by a British film). From 1983: *Local Hero* (produced by David Puttnam; Bill Forsythe's tale of a Scottish community resisting the establishment of an American-financed oil refinery, was reminiscent of the best of Ealing, but with a distinctive note which was Forsythe's own); *Educating Rita* (directed by Lewis Gilbert from the play originally commissioned from Willy Russell by the Royal Shakespeare Company); *Monty Python's the Meaning of Life; The Ploughman's Lunch* (an ambitious, if perhaps not altogether successful, satire on contemporary society and its readiness to fabricate the past for current ends; the film's claim that the traditional ploughman's lunch was actually an advertiser's invention was itself such a whopping fabrication as to rather undercut the film's moral intentions, though the incorporation of scenes from the 1982 Conservative party conference had powerful impact; on the production side Goldcrest were involved, while direction was by Richard Eyre and the story by Ian McEwan); *Never Say Never Again* (splendid effects, and Sean Connery back again in the James Bond role); *Another Time, Another Place* (directed by Michael Radford, about Italian prisoners of war in 1944 Scotland). From 1984: *Those Glory Glory Days* (built round the reminiscences of a woman football

fan, written by female football journalist Julie Welch, produced
by Enigma TV/Goldcrest/Channel Four, with David Puttnam
as executive producer); *The Company of Wolves* (a truly captivating
and imaginative compilation of dream sequences and scenes
set in the contemporary world and the middle ages, drawn
from stories by Angela Carter, and with a screenplay by her
and director Neil Jordan); *The Killing Fields* (the horrors of
recent events in Cambodia; produced by Puttnam, directed by
Rowland Joffe); *A Private Function* (in the austerity days of
1947 some local bigwigs secretly and illegally fatten a pig for
the royal wedding festivities; again reminiscent of Ealing, this
had the special qualities imparted to it by Handmade Films
and a screenplay by Alan Bennett). From 1985: *Dance with a
Stranger* (the life and death of Ruth Ellis, the last woman to be
hanged in 1953; among the production companies were Goldcrest and Film Four International, with in addition considerable
American finance; directed by Mike Newell); *A Passage to India*
(backed by EMI — Warner, written, directed and partly edited
by grand old man of British cinema David Lean, from the
novel by E. M. Forster); *Steaming* (directed by Joseph Losey
from the Nell Dunn play, about women customers protesting
against the closure of their wash house); *The Frog Prince* (one of
the consistently successful 'First Love' series for Channel Four,
Puttnam was the executive producer, the script was by Posy
Simmonds, creator of a celebrated cartoon in the *Guardian*
newspaper); *Revolution* (the most expensive British flop ever, a
view of the American revolution which American audiences
decisively rejected; directed by Hudson for Goldcrest); *Defence
of the Realm* (a near-the-knuckle exposure of a scandal involving a politician; executive producer Puttnam); *My Beautiful
Launderette* (made for Channel Four, directed by Stephen Frears
from Hanif Kureishi's script about a homosexual Asian running a launderette); *A Letter to Brezhnev* (produced by two
women, Janet Goddard and Caroline Spack for Yeardream/
Film Four International, and directed by Chris Bernard, this
was an uninhibited story of two unemployed Liverpool girls,
one of whom falls in love with a Russian sailor).

After 1985 the pace eased again, but there can be no doubting
the high quality and the originality of *The Last Emperor* (produced

by Jeremy Thomas, directd by Bernardo Bertolucci), *Hope and Glory* (directed by John Boorman, reflecting his own childhood memories of wartime London), both 1986; *Mona Lisa* (in which Bob Hoskins is beautifully outmanoeuvred and exploited by a beautiful black call-girl), *Wish You Were Here* (featuring a liberated and gutsy young woman, Linda, in 1940s Britain), both 1987; and *Scandal*, (an account of the Profumo affair), 1988. Peter Greenaway added to his reputation with *Belly of An Architect* (1987), and the absolutely stunning *The Cook, the Thief, his Wife and her Lover* (1989), a modernist morality play if ever there was one. However stage designer and avant-garde film-maker Derek Jarman has claimed that compared with his own *The Last of England* (1987) Greenaway's films 'pale into conformity'.[4] Jarman argues for a cinema which 'uses the direct experiences of the author like any other art form' and gives the specific example of a Van Gogh painting of a field.[5] Certainly to make sense of Jarman's 'dream allegory' (his words) one really does require his own account of it.[6] As in earlier Jarman films explicit homosexual encounters feature prominently. Originally to be called 'Victorian Values', then 'The Dead Sea', *The Last of England* only received its final title after shooting (on a Super 8 video camera) was complete. It repays close study; yet the problem may be that a film is a film, and simply cannot be viewed under the same conditions as a Van Gogh painting.

It cannot be said that these films conform to one particular ideology, certainly not that of Thatcherism. Indeed, the recurring element of nostalgia, particularly for the war, and the immediate post-war years, may have represented a wish to recreate the era when consensus was at its noblest. *Chariots of Fire* can be interpreted in various ways, but it does at least speak for integration into the team and the nation (the leading athletes are a Jew, a Scot and an aristocrat), rather than for selfish individualism. Almost all of the films relate to something seen as specifically British; this, after all, was usually their selling point for the American market. But, of course, international influences and pressures are often also apparent. Effective control of both production and distribution was now more monopolistic than ever (Cannon had taken over the Thorne-

EMI distribution circuits); yet individualistic productions were being made and distributed. In many ways conditions were much as they had always been: whatever the current successes, one could not make confident predictions for the future. Cinema admissions were now running at one-tenth of what they had been at the end of the forties: for the time being, they seemed to be fairly stable, but all the portents from the electronic revolution were of entertainment becoming more and more home-based.

Television was now indisputably the most important single source of information and opinion on all aspects of life.[7] It is important to mention here *The South Bank Show*, written and directed by Melvyn Bragg, launched by London Weekend Television in 1978, and replacing the earlier arts programme *Aquarius*. Bragg figures as one of the leading cultural 'mediators' of the time, but his choice of subject matter was often highly original, and certainly never stereotyped. Arts programmes of various sorts were to be found on BBC2 and on Channel Four, almost invariably informative, and sometimes creatively critical. These were programmes, one might say, preserving very British voices. Yet, in the large, one can see after 1977 an expansion of the American element in British programming: BBC and ITV were now quite openly seeking to bring in the kind of successful American series which could guarantee them large audiences at critical times in the programming schedules. In 1978 came the import of the lavish, more lush than life, *Dallas* series — very well done if you liked that sort of thing and could put up with the prolonged reaction shots. Many of the other series which came to assume commanding positions in the schedules did indeed have much more to commend them than simply high-quality production: *Hill Street Blues* (first imported in 1981), *Cagney and Lacey*, the first of the cops-and-robbers series where the cops were women (1982), *The A Team* (camp violence, 1983) and *L. A. Law* (1987).

Against this British television could, first, offer highly prestigious, lavishly produced series, usually embracing a considerable historical sweep. Redolent of the new role as the centre of high culture which television was now confidently claiming, was the series intended (unsuccessfully) to present every

Shakespeare play on the BBC over a six-year period. One of the most inventive and ubiquitous directors of the time, Jonathan Miller, was responsible for the middle two years during which he produced an interesting *The Taming of the Shrew*. Granada were responsible for what were perhaps the two most renowned series aiming for international prestige: *Brideshead Revisited* (1981), based on the Evelyn Waugh novel, and *The Jewel in the Crown* (1984), based on the novels by Paul Scott about the ending of the British Raj. In 1986 Thames produced *Paradise Postponed*, John Mortimer's saga of failed social change in modern Britain, while the BBC followed in 1987 with *Fortunes of War* based on *The Balkan Trilogy* (1960–5) and *The Levant Trilogy* (1977–80) by Olivia Manning, and featuring *the* actor and actress of the new age, Kenneth Branagh and Emma Thompson. Less glamorous, but more truly daring, were the series *The Boys from the Blackstuff* (launched in 1982) by Alan Bleasdale, often humorous, but, with its cast of the Liverpool unemployed, always deeply sad, and the play *Tumbledown* (1988), Charles Wood's uncompromising story of a real-life Falklands war hero who had half his brain shot away.

Superior comedy, I have already suggested, is one of the ornaments of British television. So far I have written of specially created series, but it is worth noting the role of the novelists Malcolm Bradbury and David Lodge, both of whom have had their novels converted into series commenting sharply and wittily on contemporary society. Malcolm Bradbury's account of the trendy lefty university sociologist, *The History Man* (novel 1978, television series 1981) neatly fitted the political polarization I have already described. David Lodge's *Small World* (novel 1986, television series 1988) satirized the giddy international world of academic conferences, while his *Nice Work* (novel 1988, television series 1989) was a shrewd commentary on aspects of Thatcher's Britain. The most knowing specially written television series was *Yes, Minister* (later *Yes, Prime Minister*) by Antony Jay and Jonathan Lynn, a satire on the ability of civil servants to stop anything from being done, and on the feebleness and conceit of politicians. Slightly nearer to the traditional sit com, though with some unusual twists, was the comedy of two petty crooks, *Minder* (launched in 1979), and making much of location shots of the unfashionable London which was beginning to come into fashion. The splendid mildly feminist comedy act *Wood and Walters* began in 1982. Among the many arresting features of the early sixties had been the so-called satire boom: now perhaps in direct response to the blandness of Callaghan and the uncaringness of Thatcher, there was satire of an altogether more vicious and lewder character: first *Not the Nine-o-clock News* in 1979 and then *Spitting Image* in 1984.

The advent of 'Sky', 'Satelite' and cable television (all channels for transmission rather than production) brought nothing of creative value; however the growth of independent production companies, encouraged by government legislation enforcing access to Channel 4, is worthy of note.

Notes

1 I have been greatly helped by Martyn Auty and Nick Roddick, *British Film Now* (1985); British Film Institute, 'British Film Industry' (typescript compiled by Linda Wood, 1980); and Dennis Gifford, *British Film Catalogue* (1986).

2 The top ten films as given by the *Sunday Times*, 31 December 1989, were: (1) *Crocodile Dundee* (Peter Faiman, 1986); (2) *E.T: Extra Terrestial* (Steven Spielberg, 1982); (3) *Who Framed Roger Rabbit?* (Robert Zemeckis, 1988); (4) *Indiana Jones and the Last Crusade* (Steven Spielberg, 1989); (5) *Fatal Attraction* (Adriane Lyne, 1987); (6) *The Return of the Jedi* (Richard Marquand, 1983); (7) *Ghostbusters* (Ivan Reitman, 1984); (8) *Crocodile Dundee II* (John Cornell, 1988); (9) *Batman* (Tim Burton, 1989); (10) *The Empire Strikes Back* (Irvin Kershner, 1980).

3 Robert Murphy, in Martyn Outy and Nick Roddick, *British Cinema Now* (1985), p. 44.

4 Derek Jarman in *The Last of England: Derek Jarman* (ed. David L. Hurst, 1987), p. 163.

5 Ibid., pp. 167, 169.

6 Ibid., pp. 160–215.

7 I have again drawn on Hilary Kingsley and Geoft Tibballs, *Box of Delights: the Golden Years of Television* (1989).

13 Not Without Renown: Art, Music and Architecture

Did the 'end of consensus' bring striking changes in art? The living sculptures of Gilbert and George at the end of the sixties had generally been welcomed by conceptualists as falling within the orbit of that type of art. Their Nature photo-pieces of the early seventies seemed to have much in common with Earth Art. But Gilbert and George were great publicists for their own work and very soon they began to insist that they were not of the narrow world of conceptualism but that theirs was an art of the people.

We want Our Art to speak across the barriers of knowledge directly to People about their Life and not about their knowledge of art. The 20th century has been cursed with an art that cannot be understood . . .

We say that puzzling, obscure and form-based art is decadent and a cruel denial of the Life of People.[1]

To many critics their art was merely simplistic and meritricious. The 'Life of People' seemed, particularly in the painting of the middle and later seventies, to be the life of the lavatory wall: titles ran from 'Prostitute Poof', 'Shag Stiff' and 'Wanker' to the less and less printable, the photo-pieces incorporating graffiti, photographs (sometimes of male sex organs) and red paint. Many of the photo-pieces of the eighties are built up from pictures of young men (women never feature in the paintings of Gilbert and George). As a *Guardian* article of 15

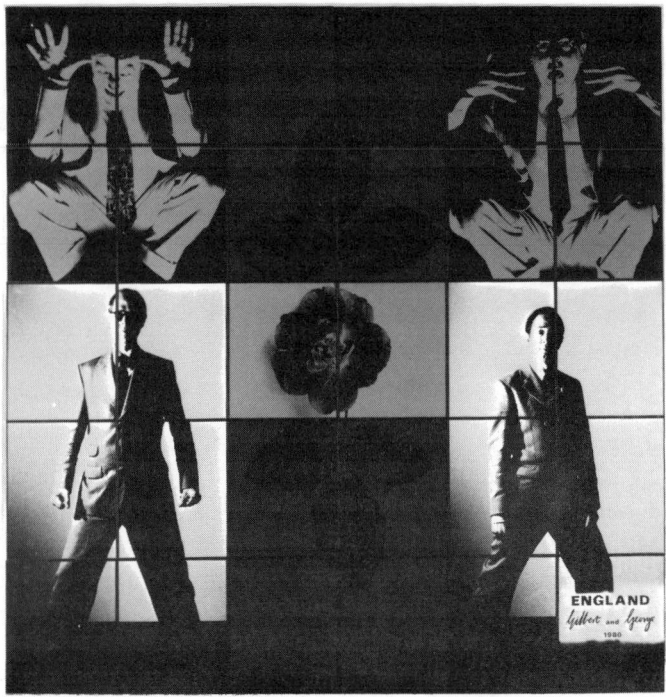

Plate 6 Gilbert and George, *England* (1980). Photopiece. 3026 × 3026 mm. Acknowledgements to the artists and the Tate Gallery.

July 1987 noted, Gilbert and George had never really been out of fashion 'but they have never been more in fashion than now'. Though they have expressed their approval of this most 'moral' prime minister, one cannot imagine Margaret Thatcher actually approving their paintings, though she may well approve their entrepreneurial spirit and populism. Their exhibition *Pictures* 1982–6, sponsored by Beck's Beer, toured Brussels, Basle, Madrid and Munich before coming to the Hayward Gallery in July 1987. Referring to the works as 'allegories of our time', the guide to this exhibition explains that Gilbert and George 'have taken the image of the youth of their world – working class, unemployed, or facing unemployment – and elevated it to the status of ideal male protagonist, of hero'.

These pictures have titles like *England* (1980, Plate 6), *Friendship, Finding God* (both 1982) and *Drunk with God* (1983).

In trying to isolate new movements, points of change and so on, it is important to take foreign influences into account. The major wave coming from America, France and Italy was that of Neo-Expressionism which, at the very least, meant a return to the use of paint. Frances Spalding identifies something of a point of change in the 1981 Royal Academy exhibition 'The New Spirit in Painting', but Fuller speaks of a new expressionistic mode 'the ugliness of which knew no bounds.'[2] For myself, I am always rather sceptical of any movement, political, historical or artistic, which is not inventive enough to call itself anything other the 'new something or other'. Be that as it may, the label we have to accept for those younger artists now happily employing paint in an expressionist manner, is 'New Image'. Sixties artist Howard Hodgkin (b. 1932), who like Rouault before him lavishly applied paint to wood to create a powerful, though intimate, emotion, was selling well, though criticized as shallow by the unbending modernists. Frank Auerbach and Leon Kossoff were now recognized as never before, with the former representing Britain in the 1986 Venice Biennale. Other painters who received a new lease of publicity were Ken Kiff (b. 1935), Gillian Ayres (b. 1930) and the Portuguese-born Paula Rego (b. 1934). Reviewing Rego's exhibition of more than twenty years of paintings, Germaine Greer described her as having a power which is 'undeniably, obviously, triumphantly female'.[3] The new emphasis was very much in keeping with the colourist and expressionist traditions which had long existed in Scotland. Links with the 1960s are provided by Sir Robin Philipson and John Bellany (b. 1942; see Plate 7): among the younger painters who now received recognition were Steven Campbell (b. 1954), Adrian Viszniewski (b. 1958), Stephen Conroy and Ken Currie (b. 1960), whose highly expressive work is clearly influenced by the social and industrial plight of Glasgow.

A perhaps even more banal label than the one I mentioned above is the 'New British Sculpture'. This is usually taken as having been announced by the exhibition 'Objects and Sculpture', held jointly at the ICA and the Arnolfini Gallery,

Bristol, in 1981, which comprised works by Richard Deacon, Antony Gormley, Anish Kapoor and Bill Woodrow. It had been preceded by an exhibition by Tony Cragg (whose bas-relief *Britain Seen from the North* of 1981, now in the Tate, 'a deconstructed school-atlas image made up of colourful plastic fragments',[4] was one of the most publicized art works of the decade) at the Whitechapel, and was succeeded by one at

Plate 7   John Bellany, *Celtic Marriage* (1978). Oil on canvas. 2540 × 1270 mm. Acknowledgments to the artist and the Tate Gallery.

Kettle's Yard Gallery, Cambridge, featuring Shirazeh Houshiary and Alison Fielding. This school can be linked both to the international revival in expressionism, and to a general return to figuration and traditional materials. The catalogue for the 'Objects and Sculpture' exhibition 'stressed that the referential had gained precedence over the formalist, and that associational rather than didactic or interrogative means were employed to elicit this content ...,' while Kapoor declared: 'I have no formal concerns. I don't wish to make sculpture about form – it doesn't really interest me. I wish to make sculpture about belief, or about passion, about experience, that is, outside of material concern.'

The least demanding of these 'new sculptors' was the new Barry Flanagan, who after 1979 took to producing appealing bronze animals of a (to say the least) distinctly conservative cast, as for example, the famous *Leaping Hare* (1981 – the sort of work that makes one want to cry 'Come back Anthony Caro, all is forgiven'). However, the new work of Richard Deacon was a little more 'difficult', containing elements of that humour which had been apparent in the sixties, but which had been rather suppressed in the troubled seventies. His constructions made of banal materials with the joins deliberately obvious, and given clichéd, or sometimes punning titles, took two directions.[5] On the one hand were solidly built objects with openings into them, for example *If the Shoe Fits* (1981) and *Out of the House* (1983); on the other 'skinlike hollow shells pierced by one or more openings'[6], such as *The Eye Has It* (1984), or *Listening to Reason* (1986). One may well detect a relationship between the works of Flanagan and Deacon and political Conservatism. Among the leading patrons of some new expressionist art and some of the new sculpture have been the Saatchis, famous as the public relations agency to the Conservative party. However, there is also a very strong sense of political commitment in some of the later new sculpture, particularly manifest in the work of Bill Woodrow. Woodrow's eighties phase began with his cutting up of discarded functional objects, combining the pieces in non-functional 'sculpture'. His move after 1983 towards supporting progressive causes can be seen in his *Life on Earth* (1984), a major large-scale installation in which he used elements (a washing machine and armchairs) he often employed for other purposes to express his concern about the threat of nuclear disaster. Depicting a family-room scene of showing home movies, the projector is placed on top of a washing machine from which it itself is fabricated. Film spills on to the floor toward the screen which is made out of part of the coverings of the five armchairs representing the absent family. While at once an under-water scene of a reef, the image on the screen also depicts a mushroom cloud (its scale indicated by the tiny palm tree at the bottom centre) with undersea creatures thrown up into the air; here is both the chaotic origin and cataclysmic demise of life on earth.[7]

The transition is apparent in *Car Door, Ironing Board, Twin-Tub, with North American Indian Head-Dress* (1981, Plate 8).

That it is impossible to speak of any one school of art, or any one ideology, dominating in the eighties is made clear simply by considering the titles and content of the major exhibitions. In 1988 and 1989 there were exhibitions of Rego and Bellany (at the Serpentine), of Michael Craig-Martin (the supreme conceptualist, now producing neat, witty, sculptures, nicely integrated in comparison with his messy boxes and pulleys of the seventies) at the Whitechapel, and a commercial show by Caro, now more figurative, certainly, than in his revolutionary days. Candidates for the sixth Turner prize included Lucien Freud, Paula Rego, Richard Wilson (Temporal, Site-Specific installations) and Richard Long (Land Art). It is probably true that Britain's reputation abroad depends most on a handful of truly individualistic artists whose reputations go back well before the eighties, (and, usually, the seventies) — Bacon, Freud, Auerbach, Kitaj, Hockney, etc. Labels sell paintings, so for some of these the title 'London School' was revived.

Much the same is true with 'serious' music. The tension between modernism and traditionalism continued. The most extreme modernist of the latest generation is Brian Ferneyhough, upon whom the influences are exclusively continental. His music is probably still not widely known in Britain, but he fits into this chapter since the point which brought him to the attention of knowledgeable British audiences was the recording in 1977 by the London Sinfponietta of his *Transit* for voices and chamber orchestra. Paul Griffiths stresses the international

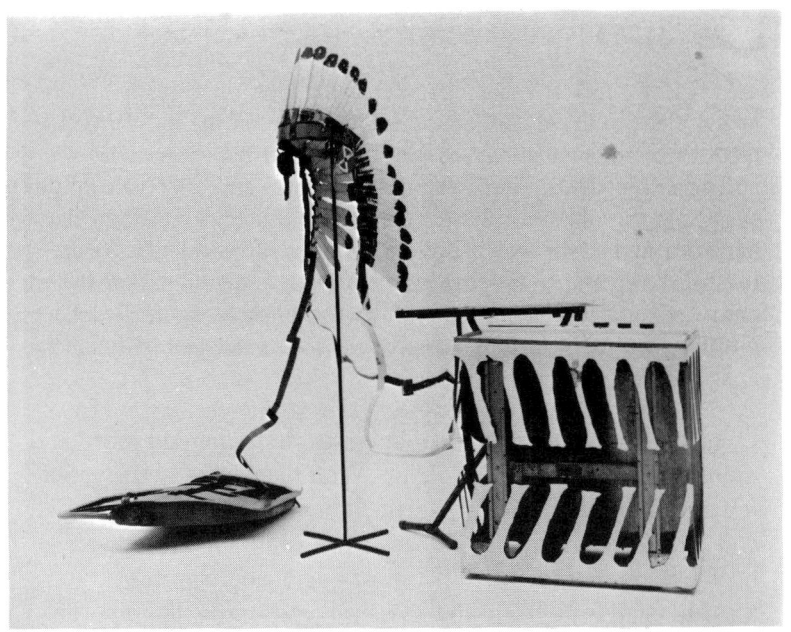

Plate 8   Bill Woodrow, *Car Door, Ironing Board, Twin-Tub, with North American Indian Head-Dress* (1981). Sculpture in various materials. 1860 mm. × variable distance. Acknowledgements to the artist and the Tate Gallery.

character of recent British composers, simply noting that Nigel Osborne has been eager to work closely with contemporary English poets, including Craig Raine, the librettist of his opera *The Electrification of the Soviet Union*, which was presented at the Royal Opera House in 1987. A year previously *The Mask of Orpheus* by Harrison Birtwhistle had been premiered by the English National Opera. This work includes electronic music which had been taped at the computer music laboratory in Paris directed by Pierre Boulez. Griffiths describes *The Mask of Orpheus* as follows:

it is a tangle of tellings of the most venerable operatic myth, not quoting from Monteverdi, Gluck, and the rest, but contributing a late twentieth-century view, in which different accounts of events are sung, mimed and acted in a complex of simultaneous alternatives, successive changes and interleaved allusions. Each of the central characters has three incarnations on stage, and sometimes all three are present; there are also mimed enactment of other, related myths, taking place to the electronic music that is one of the most inventive features of an abundantly rich score that otherwise emphasises wind and percussion. It is the increasing knottedness and complexity of the skein of stories that provides the opera's dynamic, not any particularly narrative, and so the work discovers a means of providing a coherent theatrical experience without the equation between narrative and harmonic progression through which the birth of opera had been possible, and to which it has almost always seemed indissolubly linked.[8]

As subsidies were reduced, opera came to depend more and more on commercial sponsorship. With the advent of the yuppie it came more and more to seem the entertainment of the rich and privileged. Expensive seats were often in the service of business entertainment. What most opera-goers preferred were the old standbys from the classical and romantic repertory. Yet it would certainly be unimaginative to dismiss some of the marvellously inventive productions of Opera Factory (particularly their *Così fan tutte* set in modern dress on a sybaritic beach), Scottish Opera, Welsh National Opera, the English National Opera (particularly Jonathan Miller's 1940s *Rigoletto*, and a *Cav and Pag* transferred to industrializing Italy and presented as if two parts of the same opera)[9] and, indeed, of the Royal Opera House. And it would be mean-spirited not to recognize that the opera renaissance – aided by TV and recordings – went well beyond the land of yuppies and snobs, as, for example, the success of Opera North would testify. Television productions had always had sub-titles to help overcome the problem that most of the standard operas are in a foreign language: electronic innovation and the search for audience appeal brought surtitles to the Royal Opera House in the eighties.

'Experimental music', 'neo-Romanticism', 'minimalism' are key phrases in orchestral and chamber music: the cross-fertilization between popular and classical music initiated in the sixties continued. Yet accounts of art music inevitably leave out Andrew Lloyd Webber: the musical, of course, is neither pop nor opera. Lloyd Webber's immense success with such shows as *Evita* and *Cats* certainly deserves to be noted. On the pop, or rock, front it cannot be said that there were any startling departures from the lines laid down in the sixties. On the one hand the possibilities of electronic synthesizers grew ever more sophisticated, on the other the major distinctive movement purporting to challenge the status quo in the pop world was Punk Rock, which first hit the headlines in 1976. The punks deliberately used cheap equipment, while aiming to give themselves a frightening, even vicious, image and appearance.[10] Aspects of popular music clearly are implicated not only with movements among the masses but in intellectual changes. Poststructuralism, linguistic materialism and feminism were all throwing doubt on the nature of sexual identity: two of the most glamorous pop stars of the 1980s both presented an image of deep sexual ambiguity, the American Michael Jackson, and the Englishman Boy George (leader of the group Culture Club). On the whole, in terms of international reputation, British pop music held closer to the reputation of television than to that of film. In March 1984 the *Observer* was reporting that 'Britain has returned to its customary position as the world leader in pop music'. The groups singled out at that time (the occasion was the annual American Grammy Awards) were The Police, Duran Duran and Culture Club. Unkind comments were made about the musical talents of Irishman Bob Geldof, but he certainly, and very deservedly, held centre stage for his notion of Band Aid, using popular performers to raise money for the starving in Ethiopia. In March 1985 *Rolling Stone* nominated the Dublin group U2 as 'band of the eighties'. In April 1987 U2 appeared on the cover of *Time* (only the Beatles and The Who had managed this previously). Their album *The Joshua Tree*, released in March 1987, quickly went to the top of the album charts in both the UK and the United States. The point to bring out here is that in pop music, no more than in art and sculpture, can one detect a consistent ideology, still less a Thatcherite one: U2 songs were distinguished by a strong element of social criticism and political protest.

Perhaps in some kind of distant echo of polarization in politics, architecture was characterized by two rather different, even opposed, phenomena. Within the world of the élite Britain was suddenly scoring international success because of the work of a tiny group of 'high-tec' architects, of whom the doyen was James Stirling, some of whose earlier work I have already discussed. In 1958 Stirling had written, 'one has only to compare the Crystal Palace to the Festival of Britain, or the Victorian railway stations to recent airports, to appreciate the desperate situation of our technical inventiveness today, compared to the supreme position which we held in the last century'. It is not entirely irrelevant, though slightly at odds with the polarization image I have just suggested, to recall here that Margaret Thatcher herself put great faith in the restoration of Victorian values.

The first intimation that we had a world-status architect among us came as the Beaubourg Centre in Paris was completed in 1977, the architect being Richard Rogers, born in Florence in 1933 of Anglo-Italian parents. The third of what very much came to be thought of as a trio, Norman Foster (born in 1935 into a very modest Manchester milieu), completed the Sainsbury Centre for the Visual Arts at the university of East Anglia in the same year; unassailable international reknown came with his commission for the Headquarters for the Hong Kong and Shanghai Corporation, a much-discussed and unmissable feature of the Hong Kong waterfront, consummated in 1986. *The* architectural event was the completion in 1986 of the new Lloyds of London, to the design of Richard Rogers. The analogy of the meccano set has been applied to both this building and the Beaubourg. Rogers likes to speak of 'served' and 'servant' spaces: he has said of the Lloyds building, 'whereas the frame of the building has a long life expectancy, the servant areas, filled with mechanical equipment, have an extremely short life, especially in this energy critical period'. Architectural historian Deyan Sudjic has explained that the building is

an arrangement that will allow for any foreseeable growth to be accommodated without compromising the single-space underwriting room. The centre of the building is a twelve-storey high barrel-vaulted atrium that rises up through the middle of a series of regular rectangular office floors . . . The underwriting room is on the principal floor, just above street level, and future growth will take place by spilling over the lower levels of office space around the atrium, which is criss-crossed by escalators. Surrounding the atrium are six towers, containing lifts, stairs, washrooms and service ducts. The towers are expressed as the dominant elements in the overall composition ...[11]

Most admired among the younger generation of 'high-tec' architects were Nicholas Grimshaw and Richard Horden. Grimshaw's most notable work was his Sainsbury's superstore in Camden Town together with his high-tec housing overlooking the nearby canal. One modernist (but not high-tec) work which did manage on the whole to escape controversy was Barry Gasson's museum, perfectly designed in a park to the south of Glasgow, to house the Burrell Collection of paintings and art objects.

With respect to the other cultural developments discussed in this book I believe that native British traditions or innovativeness, or on the other hand general international trends, have been far more important than specifically American influences. However, there can be no doubt as to the American dimension to 'high-tec' architecture: it is most significant that Stirling, Rogers and Foster all spent time in America − in the words of Sudjic, 'America alone seemed able to pursue technologically advanced modernism'. Near to the Lloyds building there already stood Richard Seifert's National Westminster Bank tower, a building whose major claim to attention was that at 183 metres it was Britain's highest tower block, but one without much other distinction (high-tec or otherwise) and which would have looked rather ordinary in New York or San Francisco; completed in 1981, it was, however, at least considerably more elegant than Seifert's Centre Point of ten years previously.

The other phenomenon is expressively summed up in the phrase 'heritage industry'. Whether this, or high-tec architecture, is more 'Thatcherite' would make a fine subject for analysis, for the more important consideration is that both the spirit and the end product of the heritage idea are very American. Of course, the implications of the heritage industry (the phrase derives from Robert Hewison's powerful and influential work *The Heritage Industry: British Culture in a Climate of*

Decline, 1987) extends far beyond architecture. In its architectural aspects it implies conserving the old, or building in styles designed to simulate the old. With the awful example of the redevelopment of the fifties and sixties still before everyone's eyes, the former could scarcely be thought to be anything but good; the latter was more open to criticism. In fact the struggles between modernists and traditionalists became news in a way in which similar struggles within the other arts simply did not (architecture, as I have already noted, is both élite art, and the art which most affects the public), with the traditionalists led by the Prince of Wales, who was successful in preventing what he termed 'this monstrous carbuncle' being built as an extension to the National Gallery. Careful attention to that debate, I believe, demonstrates the validity of what in effect has been a sub-theme of this book: that to perceive all cultural practice in terms of an antithesis between modernity and traditionalism is to miss the interactive and iterative nature of all living culture, just as to condemn all art which does not swallow modernism whole is to fail in both aesthetic and historical sensibility.

Notes

1 *Gilbert and George: The Complete Pictures 1971–1985* (1986), p. VII.
2 Frances Spalding, *British Art since 1900* (1986), p. 232; Peter Fuller, 'The Visual Arts', in *The Cambridge Guide to the Arts in Britain: Since the Second World War* (ed. Boris Ford, 1988), p. 116.
3 *Modern Painters*, Easter 1989.
4 William Feaver *Observer*, 24 December 1989.
5 Mary Jane Jacob, 'Richard Deacon: the skin of sculpture', in Terry A. Neff (ed.), *A Quiet Revolution: British Sculpture since 1965* (1987), pp. 74–6.
6 Ibid., p. 74.
7 Mary Jane Jacob 'Bill Woodrow: objects reincarnated', in Neff, *Quiet Revolution*, p. 160.
8 Paul Griffths, Music; in Ford, *Cambridge Guide to the Arts*, p. 74.

9 I personally was apalled by David Pountney's 'post-modernist' production of *A Masked Ball*, though in the end, fortunately, Verdi, the orchestra and the singers triumphed over the daft attempt to give the opera a Marxist message.

10 In general see Dave Laing, *One Chord Wonders: Power and Meaning in Punk Rock* (1985).

11 Deyan Sudjic, *Norman Foster, Richard Rogers, James Stirling: New Directions in British Architecture* (1986), p. 179.

14 From Ink to Inc.

The purpose of this perhaps inappropriately tricksy title is to emphasize the great changes in book publishing which took place in this era of increased commercialism and the abandonment of the intellectual standards associated with the great and the good of the consensus era. It often used to be said that the reason why there were always more aspiring novelists than artists or architects was that all you needed to get started was paper, pen and ink. You might not make much money, but if you had talent you would at least make it into print. By the later eighties, it was claimed, the dominance of American corporations and American attitudes meant that there was no longer a search for unique new talent, only for blockbusting best-sellers. There were, in fact, about ten major combines dominating British publishing. The once highly independent Secker and Warburg (they had taken on Orwell's *Animal Farm* after Gollancz, Faber and Cape had all found it too hot to handle) were now, along with Heinemann, and the general and fiction sections of Methuen, part of Reed International. Methuen's academic books were amalgamated with Routledge, which belongs to International Thomson. Hutchinson, Cape, Chatto and Windus and the Bodley Head had all been merged into Random House, itself a mere fragment in the RCA conglomerate. Collins were owned by Rupert Murdoch's News Corporation; Penguin, Longman, Hamish Hamilton and Michael Joseph by the Pearson Group.

The potential loss of independence and individuality in choosing books for publication is one aspect of this process of take-over and conglomeration. Another is that the massive corporations have financial resources which the remaining small publishers simply cannot match. 'Stripped down to essentials,' as John Sutherland puts it, 'publishers have one function – the provision of risk capital for the books of their choice.[1]

The potency of the new conglomerated publishers is the vast reserves of money (in the form of guaranteed overdraft) available to them for authors' advances. List-building nowadays requires very deep pockets. The million dollars (they called it £650,000) which Chatto advanced Michael Holroyd for his unwritten and distant biography of Shaw was no aberration. These are the sums and time-scales in terms of which publishers and ambitious authors must now think. Newly set-up publishers with the bank manager breathing down their neck, and the surviving independents with modest annual turnovers, may well discover new talent as they always have in the past. But they will have great difficulty in holding on to that talent.[2]

Author loyalty, Sutherland continues, can often be strong 'but is rarely strong enough to withstand six-figure inducements'. 'Small independent publishers will become like Fourth Division football clubs, forever losing their stars at the first gleaming. The same is true of managerial talent.' Sutherland comments that there is something logical in the feminist publisher Carmen Callil, who developed Virago to publish women's books, 'going on to tycoon status at Chatto.'

As with book production, so with bookselling. Waterstones and Pentos (owners of Dillons) had already introduced a rudimentary form of the chain-store system which dominates in America. Most recently, Waterstones have been taken over by W. H. Smith, the most venerable British chain-store of all. W. H. Smith have already accused Waterstones of 'over stocking', a revelation of chain-store policy of holding only relatively few titles and aiming to shift them as quickly as possible. Other features of this form of retailing are massive front-of-store displays allocated to hand-picked books of the day, a strong emphasis on best-selling and 'newly published' items, and on 'a dozen or so easily racked categories such as "how-to" books, fiction, health books, children's books, biography'.[3] New retailing methods are combined with new spheres of advertising. In chapter 8 I noted the significance of the 'charts' in marketing pop records; Sutherland points out that the first reliable weekly best-seller list for books in Britain was set up by the *Sunday Times* in the mid seventies, that such lists are widely prevalent, that the quality papers now devote more pages than ever before to book reviews, and that the basic purpose of this is to attract advertisements from the big book publishers. Currently the Net Book Agreement protects small independent bookshops endeavouring to hold a wide stock of books (rather than simply concentrating on best-sellers). Pressure to abolish this system, thus making it possible to further stimulate sales of best-sellers by cutting their prices, and also to get rid of slow-sellers at give-away prices, led by Terry Maher, chairman of Pentos, was intensifying as I completed these pages.

The purpose here is simply to summarize the most important changes in the production and marketing of books. It may well be that there is force in the argument that during the era of consensus too many books were published. It has also to be noted that some new independent publishers were appearing, and sometimes surviving. It would certainly be wrong to assert that the marketing of books was becoming *just like* the marketing of hamburgers or of personal computers. The more accurate comparison would be with popular records and popular theatrical events: the latter parallel is brought to mind by the appearance along the sides of London buses of advertisements for Martin Amis's novel *London Fields*. The concept of prizes for cultural endeavour is an old and hallowed one, certainly with roots in the metropolises of old Europe as much as in brash America. It may reasonably be said that such literary prizes as the Booker and the Whitbread serve the valuable purpose of stimulating interest in at least a limited number of novels of high quality; at the same time literary prizes have tended to take their place along with many other devices and many other mediating influences in the incorporated business that book publishing has become.

What of the product? In September 1989 the literary critic D. J. Taylor published a harsh attack on the state of British fiction and the literary establishment which sustained it, *A Vain Conceit: British Fiction in the 1980s*. In an article in the *Observer*, Blake Morrison reflected:

A writing of half-tones and gentle quietism, full of Hampstead twitter and coy self-examination, a writing with the significance and contemporaneity of old-time musical hall or a Punch and Judy show: there can be few of us who don't sometimes feel all this to be true of the English novel.[4]

Morrison then, however, went on to suggest that, if nothing else, that year's Booker short list 'might almost have been deliberately assembled to display diversity and balance'. Referring to Margaret Attwood's *Cat's Eye*, John Banville's *The Book of Evidence*, Sybille Bedford's *Jigsaw*, Kazuo Ishiguro's *The Remains of the Day* (the eventual winner), James Kelman's *A Disaffection* and Rose Tremaine's *Restoration*, he summarized the authors as: 'a Canadian, an Irishman, an Anglo-Japanese, a Scot, an English Rose and a cosmopolitan Sybille; three men, three women; two novels from independent houses, four from independent-conglomerates; an age-span from 35 to 78 . . .'.

Britain had no practioners of the *nouveau roman*, but then the ones the French had were not universally admired by French critics.[5] It will, I hope, have become clear to readers (should they ever have doubted this) that there is no one test of modernism which can be applied to cultural artefacts. What would be 'un-modern' in a novel would be the attempt at complete illusionism, the attempt to make the reader feel that he or she has somehow (and part of the illusion is that the reader does not question this 'somehow') become privy to real events and real behaviour, magically filtered (so magically, that the reader again is not aware of the magic) so that only those elements which (eventually) contribute to a coherent and satisfying story are presented. To be in some sense modern is to eschew sacrificing everything to the coherence of the plot, to acknowledge that the novel is an artificial literary construct, to introduce techniques borrowed from other cultural practices (film, poetry, opera, advertising, for instance), to indulge a preoccupation with the very nature of art or culture, to, in the interests of a more immediate realism, break the conventions of what was previously considered to be acceptable (with respect, say, to how women are supposed to think or act, to sexuality, to bodily functions, to drugs, to how children and adolescents and the racially underprivileged perceive the world, etc., etc), to avoid the *juste milieu* in favour, say, of pushing the latest discoveries of science, the latest theories of language to their furthest extremes, or, on the contrary, resorting to the most highly distilled understatement: all or any of these.

Perhaps one may best start this final glance at the British novel by considering the Amis's K. and M. In *Money*, which is narrated in a highly personal, and sometimes dishonest, way, by yuppy advertising agent and pornographic film-maker John Self, Martin Amis introduces *himself* as a minor character. Self, who has all the crude cynicism and jealousy of you and me, remarks to M. Amis: 'Your Dad, is a writer too, isn't he? Bet that made it easier.' To this M. Amis replies: 'Oh, sure. It's just like taking over the family pub.'[6] There may be a family resemblance in the grouchy, self-preoccupied wit: however, K. Amis has made clear his unease with his son's literary development, while such critics as D. J. Taylor admire Martin, but reject Kingsley as representing the old guard. I have already suggested that *Dead Babies*, a very concentrated book, anticipates, in a highly coloured way, some aspects of the Thatcherite world. To say that *Money* is set within that world would be ludicrously limiting, though there is contemporary relevance in the manner in which the action is divided between London, New York and California. The novel is subtitled 'A Suicide Note', addressed, says the author in a brief note at the beginning of the book (but 'there are more suicide notes than there are suicides') to 'you out there the dear, the gentle'. John Self has his shafts of deeper illumination:

Look at my life. I know what you're thinking. You're thinking: But it's terrific!
It's great!
You're thinking: Some guys have all the luck!

Well, I suppose it must look quite cool, what with the aeroplane tickets and the restaurants, the cabs, the film stars, Selina [girlfriend], the Fiasco [posh car that never works], the money. But my life is also my private culture − that's what I'm showing you, after all, that's what I'm letting you into, my private culture. And I mean *look* at my private culture. Look at the state of it. It really isn't very nice in here. And that is why I long to burst out of the world of money and into − into what?

Into the world of thought and fascination. How do I get there?

Tell me, please. I'll never make it by myself. I just don't know the way?

Since *Dead Babies*, Amis's other novels have been *Success, Other People: A Mystery Story* (which J. G. Ballard described as 'a metaphysical thriller, Kafka reshot in the style of *Pyscho*'), and *London Fields* (1989), which with Dickensian wit and energy excoriates the bad society within a perilously threatened world: 'It takes all kinds to make a world. It takes only one kind to unmake it.' As already noted, this book got on to the sides of London buses, but not into the Booker shortlist. It is said that feminists find Amis disgracefully male chauvinist: it may be that they are making that elementary mistake of confusing characters with author − John Self certainly is a male chauvinist, but we are scarcely made to feel that we ought to admire him.

As everyone knows Salman Rushdie has had sentence of death pronounced against him by the Ayatollah Khomeini for alleged blasphemy in *The Satanic Verses* (1988). Rushdie (b. 1947) provides no easy read carefully interspersed with delicious shocks. Indeed, he has been associated with that brand of modernism which goes back to 1920s Germany called 'magic realism'.

Magic realist novels and stories have, typically, a strong narrative drive, in which the recognizably realistic mingles with the unexpected and the inexplicable, and in which elements of dream, fairy-story, or mythology combine with the everyday, often in a mosaic or kaleidoscopic pattern of refraction and recurrence.[8]

Rushdie's other novels also in some way or another concerned with the tensions between Indian origins and subsequent life in the British intelligentsia, are *Grimus, Midnight's Children* (1981) and *Shame* (1983).[9]

J. G. Ballard (1930) has already been mentioned in connection with the 'new wave' science fiction of the sixties. His novel of 1984, *Empire of the Sun*, marked a new departure. As Ballard himself explained in a preparatory note, the novel 'draws on my experiences in Shanghai, China, during the Second World War, and in Lunghua C.A.C. (Civilian Assembly Centre) where I was interned from 1942—45. For the most part this novel is based on events I observed during the Japanese occupation of Shanghai, and within the camp at Lunghua.' Winner of the 1984 Booker prize, *Empire of the Sun* was recognized by Angela Carter as perhaps 'that great British novel about the last war for which we have had to wait forty-odd years': 'Significantly enough, there are no heroics — scarcely any combatants, in fact. Only a British schoolboy lost in Shanghai when the Japanese invade, a vast company doomed, Shanghai itself — that "'terrible city'" — and, in the background, history working itself out'.[10] *The Day of Creation* (1987), set in central Africa, confirmed that Ballard was now, as it were, expanding geographical frontiers as he had expanded scientific ones, always with that potent, poetic imagery which had distinguished his earlier works.

In 1983 the Book Marketing Council selected Julian Barnes as one of the Best of Young British Novelists for that year. His first novel *Metroland* (1980) had won the Somerset Maugham Award in 1981. Mainly it seemed a very clever account of a very clever boyhood spent commuting on the Metropolitan line between the outer suburbs and school in central London: but as it edged into adulthood, it edged also into discussion, not so much of the nature of poetry (and sculpture), but of the nature of responses to them. The discussion, as the title suggests, was much more central to *Flaubert's Parrot*, which reached the Booker shortlist.

Not all women writers, obviously, are feminists; nor, even, do all women writers seek to present a specifically female or feminine sensibility. Probably all three of these characteristics feature in some degree or another in the works of Angela Carter (b. 1940); but she is also one of the earliest and most celebrated writers to be associated with 'magic realism', as in *The Infernal Desire Machines of Dr Hoffman* (1972), *Nights at the Circus* (1984) and the collections of short stories, *The Company of Wolves* (already mentioned) and *Black Venus* (1985). Her *The Passion of New Eve* (1977), set in a horrifically violent America of the near future, has a handsome predatory man captured by a women's group and subjected to an operation which turns him into a highly desirable, and vulnerable, young woman. Fay Weldon, sticking, just, within the recognizable confines of contemporary British society, continued to present grippingly interesting characters while unfolding distinctively new backgrounds. *The Life and Loves of a She-Devil* (1983), about a lumberingly ugly woman, Ruth (the She-devil of the title) who undergoes horrific plastic surgery to be turned into a beauty, was aptly described by American novelist Erica Jong as: 'A devilishly clever parable about the nature of love and the nature of power.' Something of the special style of the book can be conveyed by a couple of extracts from the opening chapter:

Mary Fisher lives in a High Tower, on the edge of the sea: she writes a great deal about the nature of love. She tells lies.

Mary Fisher is forty-three, and accustomed to love. There has always been a man around to love her, sometimes quite desperately, and she has on occasion returned this love, but never, I think, with desperation. She is a writer of romantic fiction. She tells lies to herself, and to the world.

Mary Fisher has $(US)754,300 on deposit in a bank in Cyprus, where the tax laws are lax. This is the equivalent of £502,867 sterling, 1,931,009 Deutsch Mark, 1,599,117 Swiss francs, 185,055,050 yen and so forth, it hardly matters which . . .

Mary Fisher is small and pretty and delicately formed, prone to fainting and weeping and sleeping with men while pretending that she doesn't.

Mary Fisher is loved by my husband, who is her accountant.

I love my husband and I hate Mary Fisher.[11]

The Heart of the Country (1987) managed, among other things, to sketch unforgettably the problems deserted women have with social security officials, welfare officers and bank managers. *Leader of the Band* (1988) is the sex-pot musician out of lust for whom the narrator, Star Lady Sandra, has given up her work as a famous astronomer. The new feminist star of the eighties (though many feminists hated her for her wickedly mocking ways) was the journalist Julie Burchill, whose first novel *Ambition* (1989) was more uninhibited than anything yet: the female chauvinism of the narrator Susan Street was a mirror image of the male chauvinism of John Self. In many respects the short, delicate novels of Anita Brookner, whose *Hotel Du Lac* won the Booker prize in 1984, seemed to be characterized by the traditional virtues: but it is to be noted that *Hotel Du Lac* is a novel about a novelist, while *Providence* (1982) is a novel about an academic lecturing on a novel.

For the historian primarily interested in novels as sources for changing social attitudes, often the less ambitious novels are the most helpful. *The Ice Age* (1977), by Margaret Drabble, seems less concerned with the problems and position of women than with the loss of faith in social progress based on consensus; *The Middle Ground*, in which Kate Armstrong symbolically reflects that her father, a sewage engineer, had to cope with real shit while the shit that women complain about is really little more than mother's milk, seems pervaded by Social Democratic ideas. A number of novels at this particular time evinced left-of-centre political attitudes, reactions to the profound structural weaknesses Britain was manifesting at the end of the seventies: *Daniel Martin* (1977) by John Fowles, *Autumn Manoeuvres* (1978) by Melvyn Bragg and *A Married Man* (1979) by Piers Paul Read. Far different was the territory of Kingsley Amis, who continued to be a reliable, and funny, commentator on some of the trends in trendy London. *Jake's Thing* (1978) — Jake is an Oxford don who lives in London — is frenetically savage about rampant inflation; *Stanley and the Women* (1984), as the publishers astutely remarked on the jacket flap 'is not a book that is likely to win many prizes for fairness or fashionable social attitudes'. The accents of elderly right-wing sourness were less pronounced in *The Old Devils* (1986), a comedy of the horrible business of growing old, winner of the Booker prize. Malcolm Bradbury and David Lodge I have already mentioned: Brian Appleyard has written of their belief 'that there was a kind of aesthetic gap between realism and modernism, which new writers would feel obliged to fill'.[12] Both *Small World* and *Nice Work*, it may be quickly noted, involve the reader in some of the issues of post-structuralist linguistic and literary theory: *Small World* in part employs the rapid cutting techniques of a film.

We have already encountered Peter Ackroyd as the author of *Notes for a New Culture*: following *The Great Fire of London* and *The Last Testament of Oscar Wilde* he published his third novel in 1985, *Hawksmoor*, perhaps the finest testament to the modernism he had advocated in the first book. The novel alternates between the seventeenth century and the present. In the contemporary scenes *Hawksmoor* is a detective investigating a series of deaths which have occurred in various churches, all of which, it turns out, were designed by the seventeenth-century architect Hawksksmoor. In the seventeenth-century scenes the historical Hawksmoor is named Dyer, and represented as the protagonist of medievalism. His boss, Christopher Wren, embodies the 'first modernism' of which Ackroyd had spoken in *Notes for a New Culture*. In 1987 came *Chatterton*, set in three different centuries.

It may be noted that the best-selling fictional work of the decade, like some of the most profitable films, also had 'child-appeal', though of a distinctly different type: this was *The Secret Diary of Adrian Mole* (1983) by Sue Townsend. Also on this list were two novels by Jeffrey Archer, one by thriller-writer Frederick Forsyth, one by the established woman novelist Barbara Taylor Bradford, and a first novel by an entrant into the same general terrain, *Lace* by Shirley Conran.[13]

How fared the drama in this changing world? The answer, I think, has to be 'very well indeed'. The tide which had arisen in the later fifties, spilled forward into the sixties, crashed through the seventies, flooded into the eighties. Once formed, new theatres, new companies, and new dramatic trends are easier to keep going than are analogous developments in film. The formation of new small theatres and companies, many committed strongly to the presentation of socialist plays, proceeded in the seventies. The big subsidized theatres continued their momentum too: from 1976 onwards the National Theatre had three stages at its disposal on the new South Bank site; the Royal Shakespeare Company from 1982, had two stages in the Barbican. Among committed experimental companies there was Joint Stock, founded in 1974 by Max Stafford-Clark, William Gaskill and David Hare. In the realm of ideas there were three driving edges: the hard left principles of the playwrights Howard Brenton, David Hare, David Edgar, Trevor Griffiths, Edward Bond and John Mcgrath; the new feminist drama, which, arguably, produced over fifteen years the most exciting and innovative drama; and the determination of such figures as Peter Hall, Trevor Nunn and Jonathan Miller to present the classics in arresting and persuasive ways. Howard Brenton's *The Churchill Play*, which presents contemporary Britain as a vast concentration camp, was staged first in 1975, then again in revised form in 1989. His *Romans in Britain* (1981), presented at the National Theatre, implies relationships between Roman imperialism (symbolized in a scene of homosexual rape) and the British position in Ireland. Brenton collaborated with David Hare on *Pravda* an outstanding commercial success when presented at the National Theatre in 1985. In the words of the *New York Times*: '*Pravda* is an epic comedy — part *The Front Page*, part *Arturo Ui* — in which a press baron resembling Rupert Murdoch . . . does battle with over 30 characters as he conquers Fleet Street journalism and, by implication, liberal England's soul.'[14] Hare's *A Map of the World* (1983) is concerned with the problems of the Third World, Edgar's *Maydays* (1983) those of unclear annihilation. *Valued Friends* by Stephen Jeffreys, presented at the Hampstead theatre in 1989, was a comedy about Thatcherism in the property market. Hare's *Secret Rapture* contrasted two sisters, a spiritual, caring one and a Conservative MP who seems to have lost her soul.

Caryl Churchill (b. 1938), the doyenne of feminist playwrights, had found in the sixties that the best creative outlet for an overburdened housewife was the writing of radio plays. Her first stage play, *Owners*, was presented at the Royal Court Theatre Upstairs in 1972. In 1976, in cooperation with Joint Stock, she created *Light Shining in Buckinghamshire*, about the sexual and political oppression of women in the seventeenth century, and first presented at the Traverse theatre. But the play was not merely political; it was very much in keeping with post-structuralist ideas about the non-existence of personal identity – six actors represented twenty-five characters, these characters being represented by different actors in different scenes. *Vinegar Tom*, about the persecution of witches, was created in collaboration with the new feminist drama company Monstrous Regiment, founded in 1975. In *Cloud Nine*, presented by Joint Stock at the Royal Court in 1982, actors again changed their roles, and men played women, women men. *Fen* is about oppressed women workers in the Fenlands. *Top Girls* (1982) had an all-female cast, *Softcops* (1984) had an all-male one. Blockbusting commercial success came with *Serious Money*, a satire on the stock market of eighties yuppydom, which, however, made absolutely no concessions, employing the fluid notions of sexuality and the other non-naturalistic devices of her earlier plays. Pam Gems was another of the early feminist dramatists: her *Dusa, fish, stas and vi* (1975) has already assumed a kind of classic status. Ten years later there came another memorable title: *When I was a Girl, I used to Scream and Shout*, by Sharman Macdonald, was first performed at the Bush, another of the little London theatres, in November 1984. Here are Vari and Fiona, as girls, playing 'willy games':

VARI: I was walking along the road doctor, and I suddenly realised it wasn't there. I've only got a hole. My penis must have dropped off. Can you help me?
FIONA: It'll be very sore.
VARI: I need my penis back, doctor.
FIONA: There's been a great demand this morning. You can have a red penis or a blue penis.
VARI: Blue, please.[15]

Charlotte Keatley's *My Mother Said I Never Should* was first presented at the Contact theatre, Manchester, in February 1987, being later presented at the Royal Court. The all-woman cast of four play women at different ages through their lives, and also as very young children. The feminist influence extended to the traditional West End theatre. Peter Shaffer's *Lettice and*

Lovage was really no more than an old-style well-made play, imaginatively presented, but appealing to the middle-aged American women predominating in the traditional audience by having the two main characters middle-aged women.

Theatrical opportunity and, no doubt, willingness to make considerable self-sacrifice, meant that across the eighties lively and uncompromising theatre was available throughout the country (most noticed of the new 'alternative' theatre companies was Cheek by Jowl). How far this would continue as both central and local authority funds dried up, it is impossible to say. Such a prestigious house as the Hampstead theatre had, for instance, depended on joint funding from the Arts Council, the Greater London Council, and the Borough of Camden; like other theatres it had to begin to enlist other help, including (significantly), the Thames Television playwright scheme. Yet, if innovation continued, it had to be recognized that all the leading playwrights were getting older and indeed really owed their careers to the more auspicious circumstances of the seventies. Classical plays imaginatively staged were attractions both for tourists and serious domestic theatre-goers. The sensation of 1984 was Anthony Sher's portrayal of Richard III at Stratford-upon-Avon as a 'bottled spider', an embittered cripple on crutches. The most-talked of actor at the end of the decade was Kenneth Branagh, who having first set himself up as an actor-manager, then went on to a direct challenge of Olivier with his own film of *Henry V* – a Pre-Raphaelite blend of *Chariots of Fire* and *The Long Good Friday*.

Fashion in poetry fluctuated more sharply than it had done in drama. The newest poetry of the 1980s was characterized by a flight from the intimately personal, and the absence of any strong political commitment, a slightly paraodixical phenomen given that, by general consent, the most important and influential poet of the period is Seamus Heaney, whose poetry evidently has roots, however deeply they delve, in the troubles of Northern Ireland. In their introduction to the *Penguin Book of Contemporary British Poetry*, Blake Morrison and Andrew Motion use a phrase from Heaney's poem, 'Exposure', 'inner emigrés': 'not inhabitants of their own lives so much as intrigued observers, not victims but onlookers, not poets working in a confessional white heat but dramatists and story-tellers.'[16] The point, the editors say, is that

> as a way of making the familiar strange again, they have exchanged the received idea of the poet as the person-next-door or knowing insider, for the attitude of the antropologist or alien invader or remembering exile . . . It is a change of outlook which expresses itself, in some poets, in a preference for metaphor and poetic bizzarerie to metonymy and plain speech; in others it is evident in a renewed narrative — that is, in describing the details and complexities of (often dramatic) incidents, as well as registering the difficulties and strategies involved in retelling them.[17]

The change from more directly political poetry is evident in the development of Heaney himself who, by the beginning of the eighties, was particularly well known for his 'Bog Poems', where the point of reference is the bodies which have been preserved in Irish peat bog, victims of the ritual sacrifices carried out by an ancient Irish civilization.

The principle of 'making the familiar strange again' came through very clearly in *A Martian Sends a Postcard Home* (1979) by Craig Raine (b. 1944). From this title there derived the name 'martian poetry', poetry whose effect depended on the familiar being described in a strangely new way, as it might be by a visitor from Mars. To quote the famous lines from 'A Martian sends a Postcard Home':

> *Only the young are allowed to suffer openly*
> *Adults go to a punishment room with water but nothing to eat.*
> *They lock the door and suffer the noises alone*
> *No one is exempt and everyone's pain has a different smell.*[18]

The 'story-telling' element of certain of the new poets is well seen in Blake Morrison's 'The Ballad of the Yorkshire Ripper', with its fabulously arresting opening:

> *Ower t'Ills o Bingley*
> *stormclouds clap an drain,*
> *like opened blood-black blisters*
> *leakin pus and pain.*

Of course, poets I have already discussed (for instance Douglas Dunn and Fleur Adcock) continued to flourish, while the older, very conservative poet C. H. Sisson gained new audiences: however, if anything, it is a traditional Toryism he evokes, certainly not the Thatcherite variety. Readers may feel that a stanza in 'Vigil & Ode for St George's Day' expresses something akin to the approach towards cultural theory espoused in this little book of mine:

> *Either the truth is what we see*
> *Or else it is not to be seen.*
> *No more is it, perhaps; that green*
> *Is grass, that tall thing is a tree.*[19]

The title poem for the collection in which this appears, 'God Bless Karl Marx!' refers to 'the theoretical gimmicks/Of Marx and others living in a library'.[20]

Notes

1 John Sutherland, 'New Ground for the Book Trade', in *London Review of Books*, 28 September 1989, p. 16.

2 Ibid.

3 Ibid.

4 *Observer*, 24 September 1989.

5 In 'Le Nouveau Roman: Qu'en reste-t-il?', *Figaro Litteraire*, 18 September 1989. The majority of contributions expressed strong hostility to 'the new novel'.

6 Martin Amis, *Money* (1984 Penguin edition, 1985), p. 88.

7 Ibid., p. 123.

8 Margaret Drabble, *The Oxford Companion to English Literature* (1985), pp. 606–7.

9 In *The Cambridge Guide to the Arts in Britain: Since the Second World War* (ed. Boris Ford, 1988), p. 204.

10 Frontispiece to the paperback edition (1985).

11 Fay Weldon, *The Life and Loves of a She-Devil* (1983), pp. 5–6.

12 Brian Appleyard, *The Pleasures of Peace: Art and Imagination in Post-war Britain* (1989), p. 331.

13 *Independent*, 30 December 1989.

14 Quoted on the back cover of Howard Brenton and David Hare, *Pravda: A Fleet Street Comedy* (1985).

15 Sharman Macdonald, *When I was a Girl, I used to Scream and Shout* ... (1985), p. 10.

16 Blake Morrison and Andrew Motion, 'Introduction' to *Penguin Book of Contemporary British Poetry* (1982).

17 Ibid.

18 The poem is printed in Morrison and Motion, Ibid., pp. 169–70.

19 C. H. Sisson, *God Bless Karl Marx!* (1987), p. 7.

20 Ibid., p. 39.

15 Conclusion: A Decent Record?

Just as I was coming to the end of my labours with this text, Paul Johnson, sixties socialist become eighties Thatcherite, published in *Modern Painters* a highly critical review of *The Cambridge Guide to the Arts in Britain: Since the Second World War* (of which I myself have made great use in this book). In this he perceptively identified five important developments in the arts in Britain since 1945, attaching questions to each one. Here are his points (denoted by italics), together with my answers:

First, there has been an explosion of state subsidy, particularly in the performing arts and above all in the theatre. What effect has this had on the quality of the art produced?

Apart from Pinter and, less certainly, Osborne, Stoppard, Churchill and Hare, there are no names to inscribe on the roll of world playwrights (recognizing that the British have no claim on Beckett). But two to five in forty years is not bad going. Far more important, British theatre from the end of the fifties has been, and continues to be, wonderfully exciting, a true enrichment of life. The inspiration, as I hope I have demonstrated, has consistently come from the subsidized companies.

Second, there has been an architectural disaster of unparalleled magnitude, which has no precedent in our history and the dimension of which we are only just beginning to grasp. How did it happen? What lessons can we learn from it?

Agreed, though as early as the sixties one can see that lessons were beginning to be learned. But, no more than any other cultural practice is architecture monolithic, subject to simplistic 'modern' versus 'traditional' judgements. San Francisco has a more effective regulatory system than do British cities. It is the étatism of a Mitterand which has provided the planned environment in which the most challenging architecture can be placed in the most appropriate sites.

The third event is the coming of TV, which is now the biggest cultural fact in the lives of perhaps 90 per cent of our people. Clearly it is a new and pervasive ingredient in all the arts. Is it malign or beneficial, or, if both, in what proportions?

Agreed, again. British television is the admiration of the world: the inspiration has come from the subsidized BBC, from carefully regulated ITV, consciously aiming at standards well above those merely dictated by the market and, in particular, from the cross-subsidized Channel Four. Television is malignant in that it encourages passivity, becomes a substitute for direct exploration of, say, the printed page or the painted canvas. But other levers can be pulled to cope with that. In far greater measure, television has been a force for the enrichment of life. We are, of course, on the verge of fatally tipping the balance the other way, of destroying all that has been achieved.

Fourth, the arts have now entered the auction-room era. Awareness of spectacular rises in prices, further stimulated by TV and the popular cult of country-house visiting, have produced enormous interest in the fine and applied arts, and have given rise to entirely new phenomena, such as the heritage industry. Again, are these developments malign or beneficial?

Once more, agreed. And one could perhaps add the matter of literary prizes and the manufacturing of best-sellers. Raising consciousness of what is authentic can only be beneficial: but where, as happens in a free market denuded of subsidized standard-bearers, the temptation for entrepreneurs to generate the inauthentic becomes irresistible, the results are malign.

Lastly, it is notable that while public interest in old masters and classical music has never been greater or more widely spread, non-figurative art and 'modern' music still lack any popular basis. Why is this, and why is it that literature, by contrast, has largely abandoned experimentalism and has reverted to traditional forms? Is it because most people can read and insist on being able to understand books, whereas they treat painting and 'serious' music as esoteric luxuries mysteriously enjoyed by their betters?

I do not agree (see chapter 14) that literature *has* abandoned experimentalism: Martin Amis, Rushdie, Angela Carter, even Lodge. I think it is probably true that taste always takes longer to catch up with innovation in music than in any other art form. I do not think the point about non-figurative art is a valid one: certainly the art schools have proved in all sorts of ways to have been the most portentous interfaces between popular and high culture. If 'the snobbery that used to exist' has in part been reinforced by the new snobberies of yuppiedom they are, at the time of writing, less pernicious I believe than those that pervaded the pre-TV, pre-Rock era.

Now I must ring down the curtain. In social planning, in political management, in channelling investment where it is needed, the performance of Britain's rulers since 1945 has been thoroughly inadequate. By contrast, in culture (élite and popular), where many initiatives really have come from below, the record has been quite a decent one. Let me end on a crassly, but unrepentantly, liberal humanist note. Who and what will be remembered in fifty years time (when you earnest students, at whom this book is primarily addressed, will still be around to collect, though I, alas, will not be around to pay out)? I put my money on (in alphabetical order more or less): Amis K. and Amis M. C. (pairs are always more easily remembered than singles); Bacon, Francis; the Beatles, Britten and Tippett; the Rolling Stones; Carter, Angela and Weldon, Fay C. (two of the most compelling of the feminist writers); Frink, Elisabeth (perhaps the most *complete* of all the artists I have discussed); Greene, Graham (evergreen in topicality and the striking of deep human chords); Pinter, Harold, and Potter, Dennis; *The Third Man; Till Death Us Do Part; The Long Good Friday; The Red Shoes*; the Lloyds building.

APPENDIX

**Television National Top Thirties for Week
Ended 14 January 1990**

BBC1	million
1 Neighbours (Fri)	19.45
2 Neighbours (Wed)	19.42
3 Neighbours	19.28
4 Neighbours (Tues)	19.17
5 Neighbours (Thurs)	19.09
6 EastEnders (Thurs/Sun)	18.85
7 EastEnders (Tues/Sun)	17.87
8 Bergerac	13.82
9 Antiques Roadshow	12.20
10 Question of Sport	12.03
11 You Rang, M'Lord	10.52
12 Porridge	10.52
13 Survivors	10.38
14 May to December	10.31
15 Six o'Clock News (Mon)	9.49
16 That's Life	9.44
17 Holiday '90	9.31
18 Six o'Clock News (Tues)	9.27
19 Paul Daniels Magic Show	9.21
20 Six o'Clock News (Fri)	9.02
21 The Clothes Show	8.69
22 Mastermind	8.66
23 Dave Allen	8.60

24	Six o'Clock News (Wed)	8.57
25	Six o'Clock News (Thurs)	8.53
26	Top of the Pops	8.46
27	Nine o'Clock News (Tues)	8.42
28	Bob's Full House	7.94
29	Waterfront Beat	7.75
30	Nine o'Clock News (Fri)	7.57

ITV		million
1	Coronation Street (Wed/Sat)	22.58
2	Coronation Street (Mon/Sat)	21.22
3	Coronation Street (Fri/Sat)	20.89
4	This is Your Life	15.65
5	For Your Eyes Only	15.22
6	Inspector Morse	15.15
7	The Bill (Thurs/Fri)	14.63
8	Blind Date	14.60
9	Watching	14.51
10	Strike it Lucky	14.04
11	Wish You Were Here?	13.67
12	Home to Roost	13.59
13	Home and Away (Mon)	13.28
14	Home and Away (Wed)	13.15
15	The Bill (Tues/Fri)	12.96
16	Home and Away (Tues)	12.89
17	Home and Away (Thurs)	12.72
18	Yellowthread Street	12.16
19	Poirol	12.16
20	Home and Away (Fri)	12.12
21	Emmerdale (Tues)	11.80
22	Two of Us	10.83
23	Stolen	10.36
24	The Adventures of Sherlock Holmes	10.05
25	Emmerdale (Thurs)	9.87
26	Concentration	9.80
27	Wish Me Luck	9.48
28	News at Ten (Thurs)	9.28

29	News (Sat)	9.15
30	Bullseye	8.95

Source: *The Listener*, 25 January 1990

Further Reading

The important thing, of course, is to read the novels, listen to the music, view the paintings, films, etc. This guide is confined to secondary works and collections containing introductory material. The expanded edition of my *British Society since 1945* (1990) covers the entire period. The most ambitious attempt to integrate the main cultural developments (though omitting music and popular culture) into a unified vision is *The Pleasures of Peace* (1989) by Bryan Appleyard. The well-known series by Robert Hewison is very informative: *Under Seige: Literary Life in London 1939−45* (1977); *In Anger: Culture in the Cold War* (1981); *Too Much: Art and Society in the Sixties 1960−75* (1986); and *The Heritage Industry: Culture in a Climate of Decline* (1988). Volume 9 of *The Cambridge Guide to the Arts in Britain*, entitled *Since the Second World War* (1988), edited by Boris Ford, is uneven but generally useful. Janet Minihan, *The Nationalisation of Culture: the Development of State Subsidies to the Arts in Great Britain* (1977) covers an important aspect efficiently. Alan Sinfield, produced his *Literature, Politics and Culture in Postwar Britain* (1989) just as I was finishing my own book: avowedly socialist, it is a prime example of linguistic materialism, yet sparkling and informative. Sara Maitland, *Very Heaven: Looking Back on the 1960s* (1987) contains illuminating reflections by women on that central decade. *The Last of England* (1987), apart from an account of the film, contains perceptive autobiographical fragments by the homosexual stage designer and film-maker, Derek Jarman.

For art, Frances Spalding, *British Art since 1900* (1986) is comprehensive and authoritative. For certain leading individual painters it can be supplemented by Sir John Rothenstein, *Modern English Painters: Wood to Hockney* (1974), and by the following standard works: John Russell, *Henry Moore* (1968); David Sylvester, *The Brutality of Fact: Interviews with Francis Bacon* (3rd edn 1987); William Buchanan, *Joan Eardley* (1976); Diane Waldman, *Anthony Caro* (1982); Lawrence Gowing, *Lucien Freud* (1984); John Ashbery, Joe Shannon, Jane Livingston and Timothy Hyman, *Kitaj: Paintings, Drawings, Pastels* (1983); Peter Webb, *Portrait of David Hockney* (1988); *Gilbert and George: the Complete Pictures 1971–85* (1986); *Elisabeth Frink Sculpture: Catalogue Raisonné* (1984). Most of the important figures are discussed in Susan Compton (ed.), *British Art in the 20th Century: The Modern Movement* (1987), the massive cataloque for the splendid 1987 Royal Academy exhibition of that title. For recent sculpture, there are authoritative individual essays in Terry A. Neff (ed.), *A Quiet Revolution: British Sculpture since 1965* (1987). For architecture, the collection edited by Peter Murray and Stephen Trombley, *Modern British Architecture since 1945* (1984) is very sound. Anthony Jackson, *The Politics of Architecture: a History of Modern Architecture in Britain* (1970) covers a longer period, but is more critical. So also is Charles Jencks, *Modern Movements in Architecture* (1973), which is world-wide in scope. Paul Thompson's section in *A History of English Architecture* (1979) by Peter Kidson, Peter Murray and Paul Thompson is reliable.

Text books of literary history abound: W. A. Robson, *Modern English Literature* (1970) is relatively painless. In volume 8 of *The New Pelican Guide to English Literature* (ed. Boris Ford), *The Present* (1983), twenty-five experts create a classic product of the Ford assembly line, including drama, poetry and the novel, though, no longer 'the present'. Important monographs on the literature of the fifties are *The Movement* (1980) by Blake Morrison, and *Success Stories: Literature and the Media in England 1950–59* (1989) by Harry Ritchie. The collections *British Poetry since 1945* (1985) edited by Edward Lucie Smith, and *Contemporary British Poetry* (1982) edited by Blake Morrison and Andrew Motion, and the *New Poetry* (1986) edited by A. Alvarez, all contain valuable editorial matter. The specialist essays in Michael Schmidt and Grevel Lindop (eds), *British Poetry since 1960* (1972) are almost uniformly excellent. For the organization of theatre (to the early seventies at least) Ronald Hayman, *The Set-Up: An Anatomy of English Theatre Today* (1973) is outstandingly helpful. For one of the most vital recent developments, Helen Keissar, *Feminist Theatre* (1984) is invaluable. Other standard works are John Elsom, *Post-War British Theatre* (rev. edn 1979) and John Bull, *New British Political Dramatists: Howard Brenton, David Hare, Trevor Griffiths and David Edgar* (1984).

On the social aspects of music a vital book is Cyril Ehrlich, *The Music Profession in Britain since the Eighteenth Century* (1985). The chapter on 'Music' by Paul Griffiths is one of the best in the *Cambridge Guide* mentioned above. For the early part of the period the final chapter of Percy M. Young, A *History of British Music* (1967) is useful; otherwise one has to go to such individual biographies as Michael Kennedy, *Britten* (1981) and Ian Kemp, *Tippett: the Composer and his Music* (1984).

Apparently slung together at random, *Superculture: American Popular Culture and Europe* (1975), edited by C. W. E. Bigsby, does not live up to its title, though Michael Watts on popular music and Jans Peter Becker on crime and spy fiction are excellent. The standard work on broadcasting is the final volume of the monumental *History of Broadcasting in the United Kingdom* by Asa Briggs, vol. 4 *Sound and Vision* (1974). For the film industry, Martyn Auty and Nick Roddick's, *British Cinema Now* (1985) in indispensable. For the films themselves, the most comprehensive coverage is in Roy Armes, *A Critical History of the British Cinema* (1979); certain important individual films are discussed in *The Best of British* (1986) by Jeffrey Richards and Anthony Aldgate. *The Media in Britain* (1983) by Jeremy Tunstall is a good general survey, while *British Broadcasting* (1972) edited by Anthony Smith has more detail. On TV programmes themselves, *Box of Delights* (1989) by Hilary Kingsley and Geoff Tibballs is extremely useful. For sixties popular music *the* serious scholarly monograph is *Pop Music and the Blues* (1972) by Richard Middleton. Also very helpful are Charlie Gillett *The Sound of the City* (rev. edn 1983) and Michael Cable, *The*

Pop Industry Inside Out (1977). For design, the standard survey is Fiona MacCarthy, *A History of British Design 1830–1970* (1979).

Index